HOME STAGING

P9-BYI-177

HOME STAGING

THE WINNING WAY TO SELL YOUR HOUSE FOR MORE MONEY

BARB SCHWARZ

WITH MARY SEEHAFER SEARS

WILEY

John Wiley & Sons, Inc.

Copyright © 2006 by Barb Schwarz and Mary Seehafer Sears. All rights reserved.

Published by John Wiley & Sons, Inc., Hoboken, New Jersey.
Published simultaneously in Canada.

No part of this publication may be reproduced, stored in a retrieval system, or transmitted in any form or by any means, electronic, mechanical, photocopying, recording, scanning, or otherwise, except as permitted under Section 107 or 108 of the 1976 United States Copyright Act, without either the prior written permission of the Publisher, or authorization through payment of the appropriate per-copy fee to the Copyright Clearance Center, Inc., 222 Rosewood Drive, Danvers, MA 01923, (978) 750-8400, fax (978) 646-8600, or on the web at www.copyright.com. Requests to the Publisher for permission should be addressed to the Permissions Department, John Wiley & Sons, Inc., 111 River Street, Hoboken, NJ 07030, (201) 748-6011, fax (201) 748-6008, or online at http://www.wiley.com/go/permissions.

Limit of Liability/Disclaimer of Warranty: While the publisher and author have used their best efforts in preparing this book, they make no representations or warranties with respect to the accuracy or completeness of the contents of this book and specifically disclaim any implied warranties of merchantability or fitness for a particular purpose. No warranty may be created or extended by sales representatives or written sales materials. The advice and strategies contained herein may not be suitable for your situation. You should consult with a professional where appropriate. Neither the publisher nor author shall be liable for any loss of profit or any other commercial damages, including but not limited to special, incidental, consequential, or other damages.

For general information on our other products and services or for technical support, please contact our Customer Care Department within the United States at (800) 762-2974, outside the United States at (317) 572-3993 or fax (317) 572-4002.

Wiley also publishes its books in a variety of electronic formats. Some content that appears in print may not be available in electronic books. For more information about Wiley products, visit our web site at www.wiley.com.

Portions of this book previously appeared in *How to List and Sell Residential Real Estate Successfully, Second Edition*, by Barb Schwarz. Copyright © 1996. Reprinted with permission of South-Western, a division of Thomson Learning: www.thomsonrights.com, fax 800-730-2215.

Stage® and Career Book® are federally registered trademarks of StagedHomes.com.

ASP, Accredited Staging Professional, ASP approved, ASPM, Accredited Staging Professional Master, IAHSP, International Association of Home Staging Professionals, STAGE IT NOW AND PAY FOR IT LATER, The Staged Home Advantage, Staged Homes, Staging University, StagedHomes.com, and IAHSP.com are trademarks of StagedHomes.com and Barb Schwarz. All rights reserved.

Cover photos by Mary DeBella, ASPM.

Library of Congress Cataloging-in-Publication Data:

Schwarz, Barb, 1944–
    Home staging : the winning way to sell your house for more money / Barb Schwarz and Mary Seehafer Sears.
        p. cm.
    ISBN-13 978-0-471-76096-2 (pbk.)
    ISBN-10 0-471-76096-X (pbk.)
    1. House selling. I. Sears, Mary Seehafer. II. Title.
    HD1379.S353 2006
    643'.12—dc22

2005031912

Printed in the United States of America.

10 9 8 7 6 5 4 3 2

I dedicate this book to the "home" inside each of us.

Put the magic of Home Staging to work for you.

Stage to Sell and Stage to Live, too!

Keep the magic alive . . .

CONTENTS

STAGING RESOURCE CENTER

ACKNOWLEDGMENTS

I am very grateful to each and every Accredited Staging Professional that I have met and those that I have yet to meet who have earned the ASP/ASPM designations through the ASP courses I offer around the country and the world. Your care, wisdom, love, and talent never cease to amaze me. Thank you for your belief in me and the world of Home Staging I have been blessed to create.

I am also so very grateful to my coauthor, Mary Sears. Your love, support, and vision have helped make this book possible. You have become my friend and a very special spirit and light in my life. Thank you from the bottom of my heart.

I extend my love and deep-felt thank-yous to Kirk Bohrer, Sharon Beck, Shell Brodnax, BJ Johnson, Terrylynn Fisher, Jennie Norris, Wendy Waselle, Kelly Murray, Bob Kenehan, Dan Skoglund, Helga Johnson, Mark Collier, Patti and Steve Smith, Shelley Wagner, Bette Vos, Brenda Hoover, Cindy Pelland, Jane Ann Lance, Judy Taylor, Karen Hettwer, Kate Hart, Kayt Kennedy, Kelly McFrederick, Linda Jenkins, Margaret Innis, Patti Walker, Wanda Hickman, Don Deasy, John Jacobi, Andrea Schwarz, Cyndy Berry, Dorm and Vickie

Cooley, Terry Diebert, Steve and April Kieburtz, Kathy Magner, Karen McKnight, Naomi Rhode, Kathleen and Terry Sullivan, Debra Waterman, Teri and Denny Hagstrom, Kent Myers, Mike and Bonnie Altenburg, Dick and Shar Kellett, Doug and Debra Jones, Rosita Perez, Jeffrey Altenburg, the real estate agents of Whidbey Island, Bellevue, WA, Seattle, WA, Portland, OR, the greater San Francisco East Bay area, and the San Jose area whom I have worked with and sold real estate with through the years, and the entire staff, marketing, and training team at StagedHomes.com and ASP Services, Inc.

I am very thankful for Debra Englander, my publisher, with John Wiley & Sons, and my agent Jim McCarthy, with Dystel and Goderich. Thank you for your belief in me, Debra, and for your vision to lead the way with my book on Home Staging. I knew we would work together the minute I saw you and the first three minutes we were together. Thank you, Jim, for all that you do to bring my passion for writing a book on Home Staging to reality.

I also extend my appreciation and gratefulness to the thousands of sellers and buyers I have had the privilege and pleasure of serving and working with through the years, Staging their homes, selling their homes, and helping them purchase new homes, too!

I thank you, my readers. For without you, there would be no need for this book. They say that it takes both the author and the reader to make a book what it can be. What the author brings to the reader is crucial, but what the reader brings to the book, too, determines how it is read. So we are a team, you and

I, as we Stage your environment wherever you live, work, or play and whether you are Staging to Sell or Staging to Live. Use these ideas to make the set of your life a better one that is more pleasing to the eye and more fun to be in. Thank you for bringing my book into your life.

BARB SCHWARZ

INTRODUCTION

Staging works! I think I have said that at least a billion times since 1972, when I invented the concept of Home Staging. It is my mission to help as many people as I can with the gift of Home Staging. Home Staging changes lives. It really does.

I was born with a love of homes, of moving things around, of having fewer things around me and with me than some people do. I've always liked to keep things neat and clean. I'm always looking for a better way to do things.

Staging is very visual. It is all about presentation. It aims to make things pleasing to the eye. Enthusiasm and passion are a part of Home Staging, too. These days I say out loud all the time, "I love this business!"—the business of Home Staging, and the business of training others to Stage. When I Stage a home for sale I know that in some small way (and in big ways, too) I am helping to change lives. Staging clearly works—look at the statistics in the charts that follow.

When one parent has to start work in another city and the rest of the family gets left behind because their house hasn't sold, that's not good. When a couple is divorcing and they can't move forward with their lives because their house won't sell,

Current Nationwide Staging Trends

Type of Home	Average Days on Market	Average Days to Sale Pending Status *after* Staging	Sold	Equity Increase
Homes listed for sale prior to Staging (These homes were not Staged for sale, listed, and did not sell. Homes were then Staged by an ASP and *sold*.)	136 days (4.5 months)	7.6 days	Up to 20 times faster than un-Staged homes	3 percent minimum or $26,000 average (as much as 50 percent and $500,000 in some markets)
Homes listed for sale after Staging (These houses were Staged by an ASP and then listed for sale.)	32–42 days	6.8 days	2–3 times faster	3 percent minimum or $26,000 average (as much as 50 percent and $500,000 in some markets)

StagedHomes.com survey of 200 homes prepared by an Accredited Staging Professional (ASP). Copyright 2006 StagedHomes.com and Jennie Norris.

that's not good, either. Even in the best scenarios, a house that doesn't sell keeps people on hold. When we Stage a house and it sells, life moves ahead. And that's the way it should be. In my Home Staging seminars, I always ask the Accredited Staging Professionals (ASPs) to sing "Row, Row, Row Your Boat," reminding them that the words aren't "Row, row, row your boat, fighting against the current." Staging is easy, it's simple,

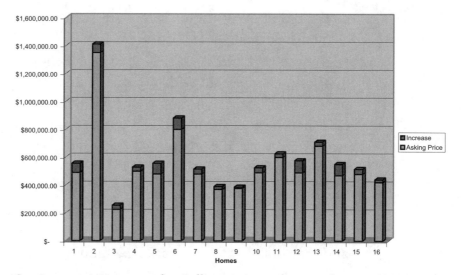

Staging can increase the selling price of your home. (2004–2005 StagedHomes.com survey of 16 homes prepared for sale by an Accredited Staging Professional [ASP] in the Sacramento area. Copyright 2006 StagedHomes.com and Jennie Norris.)

and it works. I recently Staged the home of an elderly man who received an extra $40,000 for his house. That extra money will pay for him to live another year in a very nice nursing home rather in one that is less desirable. That changes his life for the better and has an impact on the rest of the members of his family, too. That feels really good—*really* good.

Sit down, drink a cup of coffee with me, and let me tell you a story. Well, I don't drink coffee, but we could have a Diet Coke together and I will make sure that the table we are sitting at is Staged, no matter what we drink!

I have loved homes since I was very young. I used to host open houses on Sundays for the local builders in Kansas, where I grew up. I don't know where the real estate agents were. In fact, I didn't even know there were such people as real estate agents back then.

By the early 1970s, I was living in Bellevue, Washington, and feeling frustrated with my career. I had a funny feeling in my stomach and the notion that I wasn't being all that I could be. I had been a decorator and had recently made the leap to real estate on a dare from a broker I'd just met. Something made me just go and do it!

As I listed homes, I couldn't get one seller to carry out all the suggestions I made to prepare their home for sale. I'd ask the sellers to put up new wallpaper or put down new carpet, and they'd say, "You've got to be kidding me. I'm not putting another penny into this house! I'm moving! I'm selling this house as is, and the buyers can do those things when they move in." I didn't know how to respond. At that time, no one was preparing homes for sale. No one had actually thought of it. Back then, real estate agents were taught their state's real estate laws, how to prospect, how to get the listing, and how to advertise once they got the listing. You were taught how to prepare and fill out forms, but no one was teaching how to prepare property for sale. In many places it is still presumed that the seller should somehow just know what to do and how to do it. But when it comes to Home Staging, "you can't see the forest for the trees." It's hard to recognize what's around you when you live in the midst of it all the time. You get used to it. It becomes your background—your backdrop scenery—and you simply don't see it anymore.

I began to say to myself, "You are not serving these sellers with what you know would really help them." Back then, when sellers I was representing didn't want to Stage, I took the listing anyway.

Boy, have things changed since then! And if you will let me be your Staging Mama, you will not make the same mistakes that sellers often do. I will teach you to Stage. I will show you what to do, how to do it, and how to do it right the first time. I have learned so much by Staging more than 3,000 homes since I first developed the Home Staging concept in 1972, and I am learning more every day—and delighting in doing so, too!

So, what changed? What happened? How did I go from not being able to persuade any sellers to do anything to having almost every seller do exactly what I ask them to? Well, I said to myself, "Either I tell the truth and do things the right way, or I get out of the real estate industry." It is not my nature to quit, and it's not my way to back down on the things I know are right. One of the things I remember my mother saying when I was young was "Never give up," quoting Winston Churchill. It made an impression on me and is one of the most important things I remember from my childhood. So I started to stand taller and stick to my guns more often, and by doing so I set the Stage for my invention of Home Staging not long afterward.

One day I was working with a seller whose house was really a mess. I began experimenting with the way I spoke to sellers, to see which phrases worked the best. I had made the decision to not back down anymore and just accept the listing the way it looked, as I had done previously. So I said to her, "Do you like the theater?" The owner replied, "Well, yes, but what does that have to do with selling my house?" I replied, "Let's pretend your house is a 'set' on the stage of a play or a movie." I told her we needed to "Stage" her home for the audience—the buyers—who would be coming through.

I told her she was the producer, because she owned the house. And she was also the actress—the lead actress. She loved that. I also told her that I . . . well, I was her director and I would like to set the scene for how the rooms should look so that we could have a "sellout" performance, with as many people as possible coming through the house to take a look. I told her that would really happen once we cleared out the mess and straightened up. We "auditioned" pieces in different rooms and gave the house a fresh, new look.

Remember, the buyers determine how much a product will sell for. That is true in the theater and that is true when you are selling a house. Sellers believe that *they* set the price of their home when they sell it, but actually it is the marketplace that sets the price. A house is worth only what a buyer will pay for it. Another thing I've learned is that a house has two buyers: One is the buyer who eventually purchases the house, but until then, the seller is the buyer. The seller must continue to pay the mortgage—must continue buying the house—until another buyer comes along. Until a buyer steps up to the plate and pays what you are asking, you are still the buyer. You would probably never buy your house back—would you?—for the price you are asking, because you paid so much less than that when you bought it in the first place. Yet, as long as you sit there without a seller at whatever your asking price is, you are buying your own house until someone else agrees to take your place.

Some sellers so overprice their home no matter what the market is that they don't find a buyer to take their place until they lower the price. By the time they do that, they receive less than if they had priced it appropriately from the beginning. Take my advice: The audience is crucial in helping you determine whether you have priced your house correctly. They will either give you offers or simply look and keep on going. Price it right to begin with, and even more important, Stage it from the get-go. You never get a second chance to make a first impression.

So back to my story: I told this seller that we all have critics, too. They are the other real estate agents. They always talk about all the houses that are for sale. They give nicknames to the properties so they can remember the houses more easily—names like the "Pretty Red Door House" or the "Cat-Pee House." These names are either positive or negative—and why not? When there are hundreds or even thousands of houses to keep track of, how else would you remember them all? So I shared with the seller that we needed to create a positive image for the future agents to associate with the house when they came to see it, and to do that we needed to set the Stage.

The owner liked my Home Staging idea and followed through on almost everything I asked. Thus, I had Staged my first listing. The rest is history! Those few minutes in 1972 were the genesis of the entire Home Staging industry. The same principles I developed then still hold true today. In fact, the principles of Home Staging are even more relevant now, when buyers are much more demanding about what they want to buy and what they expect to see in any market. A home is one of the most important and most expensive things any of us ever buy.

The Home Staging system is now time-tested. It has helped to sell thousands, if not millions, of homes in the United States and Canada, and in several other countries as well. As the creator of Home Staging, I have never seen it *not* work. Sure, overpriced properties may sit, but it's price that holds them back, not the Staging. Two things sell a house: One is price, and the other is Home Staging. I have seen Home Staging help sell many homes that at first glance seemed overpriced, but because they were Staged, they sold. And they sold for the asking price or even more in a hot market. I promise you, if these homes hadn't been Staged, the sellers would have had to lower their price to get them sold. There is a ceiling on just how high you can go with your listing price. You should talk to your real estate agent to find out what the ceiling price in your market is.

Home Staging is not a part of the decorating industry. Some decorators have misled clients, telling them it will cost thousands of dollars to prepare their home for sale. Too many decorators want to sell too much furniture, too many pictures, and too many other items to the owner of the house, all in the name of Staging. I object! The hair on the back of my neck starts to rise when I hear things like that. This is the opposite of what needs to be done.

The goal of Staging is not to sell furniture. Selling the house and the space inside is what Home Staging is all about. Your investment is in your property. The space is what you are selling. I want to show you how Staging a home for sale can be done in easy, simple ways that work. This book is about using your creativity.

Home Staging is an important part of the real estate industry, and will be even more so in the years ahead. You Stage to Sell, and then you end up Staging to Live. The first *aha!* moment people have is that Staging helps them get more money for their house. After they see their Staged home, they understand how easy it is to live without so many things. They begin to want to live that way all the time. I call that Staging to Live. It's a process that unfolds step by step.

This book is about Home Staging and how to set the scene in your home. It isn't about spending thousands of dollars to do so.

Staging is about having fun.

Staging is about using items, accessories, and pieces of furniture in new ways. Audition things in new roles!

Staging is living life in an easier way, with less around you.

Staging is using what you have to create a new "set" in your home.

Staging is putting many extra things away.

Staging is packing those collections up early.

Staging is decluttering.

Staging is cleaning up your property.

Staging is about the colors you use inside and outside.

Staging is being committed to getting your condo, apartment, or house ready for sale.

Staging is clearing your rooms, one by one, so buyers can envision themselves living there.

No one will buy a home until they can mentally move in. That is hard to do when the rooms are full of clutter and too much furniture.

If you have a vacant property, you do need to bring furniture into the house. You need to set the scene and create what I call *vignettes* in every room, but you can rent the furniture. Our Accredited Staging Professionals (ASPs) are available to help you do that. Why would you want to buy thousands of dollars' worth of furniture when you can just rent it for the time your property is on the market, at far less cost?

My goal is to reach critical mass with the concept of Home Staging so that you and all of the consuming public realize and understand that to sell a home you should Stage it first. By doing so, your "product" will be merchandised and prepared for sale.

I have taught more than 700,000 people in my Home Staging seminars about the step-by-step process of how to Stage. I have developed the Accredited Staging Professional course and the designation of ASP for professional real estate agents and Home Stagers. I have taught them how to Stage professionally. So there is plenty of help for you wherever you live and work. I feel very good about developing a whole new industry of home-based businesses: the Home Staging industry.

Now you have my book in your hands. There is help for you in this book! There is also help available from our talented ASPs in every part of the country, who are ready, willing, and able to help you Stage your house—your product—for sale. (Go to www.StagedHomes.com to find an ASP in your area.)

Welcome to Barb's World. Miracles happen here, and they are ready to happen for you. All you have to do is believe you deserve the best. Together we will set the scene for that to happen, in your home, and in your life, too. So let's get started. Let's stage your house and your life, too!

BARB SCHWARZ
Creator of Home Staging
Real estate broker, author, president of StagedHomes.com,
Founder of the International Association of
Home Staging Professionals, and a professional speaker
who has taught Home Staging for more than
16,000 hours to more than 700,000 people worldwide.

CHAPTER 1

SO YOU'RE SELLING YOUR HOUSE . . .

STAGING IS A MIND-SET

Before you put your house on the market, make sure you really want to sell. You must begin to think of your home as your house, and your house as a product. This means letting go and moving on. I know your home is full of memories, and you don't want to leave any of them behind. But you're taking those memories with you! If you're going to sell your house and get top dollar for it, you must make it attractive, just like a box of cookies on the shelf at the grocery store. Like a product, people will be drawn to your house because it looks better than other products on the shelf.

That's where Staging comes in. Why offer your house "as is" instead of "the best it can be"? How can you expect to sell a house with scuffed walls, a dirty sink, fading wallpaper, and appliances that don't work? Even used cars are polished to

11

perfection before they're sent out to the lot. Buyers make decisions with every inch they walk. So go over your house inch by inch. Merchandise it inch by inch. Let's set the Stage!

DETAIL YOUR HOME LIKE YOU DETAIL YOUR CAR

Some people put more into selling their car than their house, even though their house is worth so much more than the car. I always ask sellers, "If you were going to sell your car, what would you do before showing it to potential buyers?" They always reply, "Wash it, wax it, vacuum it, clean out the junk, and touch up the chips." Where is most of your equity—in your car or in your house? Your house, of course. So it makes perfect sense to invest the most care in the house you want to sell for the highest possible price. However, most people don't know the secrets, tricks, and tips of Staging. They put their home on the market the way they live in it—as is. So we'll show you how to Stage it. By Staging your house, you'll immediately pull it ahead of the competition. You'll get rid of all those things that distract the buyer from the property, the walls, the building. You're selling the house, not your things, and that's the key to Home Staging.

STAGING IS NOT DECORATING

Staging is not decorating. Decorating means personalizing your space; staging is depersonalizing it. Staging is not about the ruffles you love or your favorite color rug. Staging is about getting a property sold. Decorating is optional. Staging is mandatory.

You have to get the home sold, regardless of the state of the economy. Even as the market goes up and down, the market is still going up. If you want to sell, you can only change yourself, not the buyers. What you can do is Stage your house and sell it at a profit. You want your property to look its very best so it will sell for top dollar. When you don't Stage, you are cheating yourself—and you may be losing money in the process. If you doubt this, try to flush a dollar down the toilet. Can't do it, can you? Advertising a messy house is like throwing money away. If you want to get the most money possible for your house, you owe it to yourself to Stage the property so you get top dollar.

THE PSYCHOLOGY OF THE BUYER

Buying a house can be exhausting. By the time potential buyers arrive on your doorstep, they have probably already packed and readied their own homes for sale. At this point, all they're looking for is a clean, peaceful house to purchase and move into—somewhere they can relax, feel comfortable, and make their own. Most buyers don't want to do anything to a house initially, at least for the first few months. Their energy is tapped and their resources strapped. They just want to move in and sit back for a while. Let your house be the haven they fall in love with.

THINK OF YOUR HOUSE AS A SET TO BE STAGED

In marketplace terms, your house is merchandise. In Hollywood terms, your house is the set. You're Staging it to look appealing, just like the stage set in a movie. Your favorite

> **TIP**
>
> SELLER: Now that we're leaving, we don't want to invest in this house; we want to use the money for our next house.
>
> BARB: Don't be penny wise and pound foolish. When you Stage your home, you're investing in your most important possession and earning back your equity. If your home will sell for thousands more after you buy a new sink and countertops for a few hundred dollars, you're still ahead of the game. By Staging this house, you'll have more to invest in your new home. And many Staging ideas cost nothing. That's where the creativity of Staging comes in—and it works!

television show has a set you remember and connect with. Your house is a set, too.

Consider your audience: You must appeal to the real estate agents as well as the buyers. Agents also remember only what they see, not the way it's going to be. If your house doesn't appeal to the agents, they will pass it by in favor of a house they think they can sell. If your home isn't Staged, they may use it as a comparison to a house that has been Staged. If you were a shopkeeper, you'd show your customer a gorgeous, expensive dress, not a dowdy old frock from last season. If you went into Target or Nordstrom and found a blouse you liked but the buttons were missing, you'd ask for a discount, wouldn't you? The same is true with houses. So make sure your house is Staged to be the best it can be. Be proud and confident. And let me be your director. Ready, set, Stage! On with the show!

CHAPTER 2

READY, STAGE, SELL: HOME STAGING GUIDELINES THAT WORK

PACK UP EARLY, BEFORE YOU LIST YOUR HOUSE FOR SALE

Most of us pack after we sell. But when you Stage your house for sale, it's just the opposite: I want you to pack up early, before you list the house. You're going to be packing anyway, and your house will sell faster if you pack now.

Packing early clears your rooms and makes it easy for buyers to mentally move in. No matter how lovely your things are, start packing for the next place you'll live. You don't have to pack everything, but get a head start on it. You'll be moving soon!

Rent a storage space or use a corner of the basement, the attic, or a protected crawl space or garage. (Don't put your stuff in the carport; in a Staged home, the carport is for the car and nothing else.) As a last resort, if there is a third or fourth bedroom you're not using, use it for storage. This is not ideal, but it does work. Keep the room organized, the boxes neatly stacked, and any larger items folded in the corner of the room.

Set your sights on your new house—even if you haven't bought it yet. Pack things into boxes labeled for the rooms in the new house—even if you don't know where you're moving. Pack an afghan and pillows for the den in the next place you live. Pack for the blue bedroom in your future, even if the pictures and artwork came out of your present living room. Dream about new possibilities. Think of the future. And in the meantime, work hard at Staging your house to get top dollar, so you can invest the profits in your new home, in your new location.

The way you live in your home and the way you sell your house are two different things.

This may be the best saying I have ever come up with, and, boy, is it true! The better your house shows, the faster it will sell, often for a higher price. If you're motivated to sell your house, you'll have the energy to tackle the important steps that will make it look its best. It may seem like a lot of work, but believe me, it will literally pay off in the end. So let's get started with the big three: clean, clutter, and color.

CLEAN YOUR HOUSE

Have you ever walked across a sticky kitchen floor? Me, too. I call it a "gravity pull," as in "I feel a little gravity pull here."

There's nothing more revealing than the state of your kitchen floor. It's often a clue to the cleanliness of the entire house. Clean houses are appealing. They look better, and buyers assume a clean house is well cared for. Many buyers will walk out of a dirty house without even considering what's underneath the dirt because they feel so uncomfortable. We're all so busy living our lives that sometimes we don't stop to keep our environment clean. Sometimes we don't even see the dirt. But when you sell your house, you must Stage it so it's Q-tip clean. Don't forget the baseboards, the floors, the inside and outside of the tub, the blades of the ceiling fan, the exhaust hood above the stove, and the vents in the hallway. Clean the top of the refrigerator, scour the stove, shampoo the carpets, wipe away the cobwebs in the corners of the ceiling, and really clean those bathrooms. That's just for starters.

Outside the house, power-wash the exterior walls, deck, and driveway where needed, so they're spotless. I use Krud Kutter on the driveways to get rid of grease that has dripped from cars. Paint the garage floor.

If you're one of those people who doesn't know what clean really is, ask a persnickety friend to come over and point out things that need attention. I'll never forget showing one harried mom the cookie crumbs and sticky Kool-Aid that had congealed under her kitchen cupboards. She wasn't a careless person; she was just so busy with her four kids that she'd stopped seeing the spills. Once I pointed them out to her, she went right to work obliterating the mess, thanked me, and asked for more ideas. Her house had been on the market for more than six months with another agent who hadn't guided her. She wanted to get her house sold so she could join her husband in another city, where he had started a new job. She couldn't join him until their house was sold. After Staging the house, it sold right away, and she and her kids were on their way.

A more difficult situation occurred when I was listing a house that smelled like human urine. All the other agents called it the "Pee House" and wouldn't show it. Sure enough, I found out that one of the children who lived there was a bed wetter. I approached this with the homeowner just as a doctor would sit with a patient who was about to receive bad news. I sat down with her at the kitchen table and patted her hand. I began by saying that doctors sometimes have to tell their patients difficult news, and that I had some difficult news, too, but if I didn't tell her, no one else would. Once the problem was out in the open, she quickly took care of it over the weekend by replacing the floorboards under her child's bed and buying a new mattress. The house sold the next week. I'll never forget the feeling I had at the closing when the seller thanked me for having the strength to tell her about the problem, because she really needed to sell. I was glad I was able to help her in a kindly way.

If you can smell it, you can't sell it.

Give your house the sniff test. If you have dogs, cats, hamsters, old carpeting, mildew problems, or a smoker in the house, or you enjoy cooking pungent ethnic foods, these odors must be eliminated. You may be so accustomed to these odors that you don't notice them anymore. But they're there, and agents and buyers will notice when they visit your house. Ventilate your home by opening windows on opposite ends of the house. An air-cleaning and deodorizing machine and an exhaust fan can help. Ask a friend how your house smells; you may be too used to the odor to detect it. Pet stores carry the latest products to remove and eliminate pet odors, and they don't smell worse than the problem, as they used to. Never burn candles; you may get distracted and forget them. It's best to find the source of the smell and permanently remove it. The next best solution is using one of the new products that have living enzymes in them that consume the odor-causing agents and remove the smell permanently.

Clean your carpets and curtains; the expense is well worth the price. Curtains can be removed altogether. Dark, heavy curtains or drapes can overpower a room. If there are sheers beneath, remove the curtains, pack them for the new house, and leave the sheers for privacy. This lets in light, for a fresh look.

Dirty windows are difficult to see through, and they give your house a poor image. You probably need to clean your windows anyway, so why not polish them now? Or hire a professional; they work quickly and have the equipment to get the job done.

Fireplaces need attention. Get rid of dirty ashes, and close the fireplace screen during showings. Rusted screens should be spray-painted black; hardware stores carry heat-resistant spray paint. If your house is on the market in the summer, when the fireplace is empty, put a lush plant in front of it or inside the firebox to add some greenery to the room. Remove the soot from the outside of the fireplace. Oven cleaner usually works, but test it on a small, out-of-the-way area before you use it. I use Krud Kutter on fireplaces, too. (Krud Kutter is my very favorite product, and boy, does it work, for this and so much more. Find out more about Staging and other products available from Barb Schwarz at www.StagedHomes.com.) If you can't get rid of marks on the bricks, consider painting the face of the fireplace with paint made especially for brick and stone. This makes the fireplace look bigger and better. In the right situation, I've found that semigloss white brick paint can do miracles. When I first shared this with a seller one day she thought I was out of my mind. She didn't want to do it, but her fireplace bricks looked awful. I showed her pictures of other homes I had Staged where the owners had painted the bricks. After she saw the pictures, she was willing to give it a try. She did it and got so excited about the results that she told everyone in her church to paint their bricks for a fresh new look, even if they weren't selling the home. Who knows how many fireplaces got painted that weekend?

Motivation is the engine: If you want to sell your house and get a hefty return on your investment, jump on the Staging bandwagon and get on with the cleaning. You'll find that a Staged home is easier to live in—and easier to keep clean, too!

CONQUER CLUTTER

Clutter comes home one piece at a time and eventually closes in on us. Clutter chews up energy. Clutter eats equity. Let's make your house clutter free!

A cluttered home is stressful, and in America we are cluttered to death. Clutter is one of the biggest challenges in Staging a house, but it can be conquered. You can do it—one room at a time!

Most homes come on the market with simply too much stuff in them. In the kitchen alone, there's the hot dog cooker, a hamburger press, a coffee grinder, an electric knife, a toaster, a bread maker, and a waffle iron. And that is just the beginning. Every year at holiday time it seems that another new kitchen appliance is invented. When you Stage your house, get these extra appliances out the door, or at least packed away.

When you Stage, eliminating clutter is just as important as cleaning—maybe more so. Clutter doesn't work when you sell your house. It's got to go. Remember, the way you live in your home and the way you sell your house are two different things. Buyers have to mentally move into your home for it to sell. They can't do that if your clutter is in the way. You don't want to sell your things. Take them with you and sell the space.

What is clutter? It's the stuff your spouse wants you to throw out that you refuse to part with. It's newspapers, magazines, stuffed animals, clipped recipes, china roosters, and many of the things your friends say are "so you" and "show your personality." When you Stage, hide these things. You don't have to throw out beloved clutter (though that helps), but pack away everything you don't really need (and a few things you do need but can live without) before you put your house on the market. My Staging mantra is "Less is more." You're selling your space, not your stuff. All those little tchotchkes? Pitch 'em, pack'em, but whatever you do, put them away or out of sight. The pictures on the next page tell the story.

ENERGY AND CLUTTER

I'm fascinated by quantum physics and the way it applies to Staging. All things have energy, energy involves movement, but the energy of clutter bogs us down rather than moving us

Before ASP Staging

It would be hard for any buyers to picture themselves living in this room.

After ASP Staging

Now the buyer can imagine entertaining friends in this rec room.

forward. Surrounded by the stress of a cluttered home, a buyer will shut down; as an agent, I've seen it happen many times. Buyers may say to their agent, "Show me a house in any condition; I can imagine how it will look," but most of them can't see past your stuff.

A space has its own energy, too. Buyers will stand in the doorway and feel the energy of a room. And they won't go into a room that's too cluttered because the energy is scattered. Your job is to Stage each room, which increases and concentrates the energy, and in turn draws the buyer in. Picture yourself stepping into a bright, fresh room—you know the feeling I'm talking about. Rooms speak to you—yes, they do. I assure you that I don't hear voices, but I've heard rooms say things like "Help me in here. I'm cluttered; I can't breathe." In my Staging courses, I show pictures of cluttered homes and my students moan and groan and say, "That room is drowning in stuff!" Would you like to wear all the stuff you have in your house? That's what your room is doing when it's full of clutter. The room will feel better if you empty it out so it can sell itself.

I love decluttered rooms so much that I live in a house that is Staged at all times. I call this practice Staging to Live. It is a natural progression, from Staging to Sell a home to Staging to Live, because a home without clutter feels so much better. Clutter brings stress, so a Staged home is naturally more joyous and less stressful to live in. Buyers pick up on this, too. That's why they like to buy Staged homes!

People who have a lot of belongings and face a challenge getting rid of them often have a lot of life issues as well. They aren't able to work through their life issues, so they hold on to their stuff. Once they deal with the life issues, they can let go of the clutter. If there's a lot going on in your life, this could be the perfect time to Stage, whether you're moving or not. Once you Stage, you may be in a better position to release the issues. Or release the issues and then Stage—that works, too. Since I invented Home Staging in 1972, I have seen this happen over and over again, and I have Staged more than 3,000 homes!

In my own life I just noticed that I'm in a place where I can release my grand piano. I haven't used it lately, it takes up a lot of room, and I think it will be happy moving on to a new home. Now that I've made that decision, I feel a whole lot lighter. And that decision has triggered the release of other issues in my life as well. It's interesting how this works.

Staging is seamless and fluid. When you are Staging, what doesn't work in one room may work in another. Bring the outside in and the inside out. For example, you might set a garden fountain on the ledge surrounding a big whirlpool tub.

To declutter efficiently, tackle one room at a time. Mentally toss the furniture up in the air. Play with it. You want the buyer to see space. Aim for flow and openness, so rooms look bigger. As you Stage, move everything you don't want to the doorway, where you can sort through it later. Challenge yourself to remove 100 objects from each room. Set up a tall paper leaf bag—the kind that stands up by itself—and start tossing. Pack the keepers in boxes. Give away the rest. In my experience, you can throw away more than you imagine. Open up the space for new energy to rush in. Buyers will rush in, too. A Staged home will usually sell in a shorter amount of time and for more money.

CLUTTER IS

Indoor Clutter

Too many books.

Clothes lying around a room.

Knickknacks.

Too many plants.

Too many pieces of furniture in a
room.

Too many accessories dominating
a room.

Newspaper clippings, favorite
articles you've never read.

Too many kitchen appliances on
the counters.

All those stacked magazines.

Papers on the kitchen desk.

Papers in your home office.

Messy bookcases.

Shoes left out.

Jewelry left out.

Too many family pictures (sorry—
buyers don't care about your
family pictures).

Too many throw pillows.

Too many quilts or throws in rooms.

Outdoor Clutter

Too much patio furniture.

Too many plants on patios and decks.

Old barbecue equipment.

Lawn mowers, rakes, shovels, and
tools left outside.

Dead plants in the yard.

Plants not yet planted, in those
black plastic pots.

Unused building blocks and stepping
stones.

Paint cans.

Fertilizer bags.

GUILTY OF TOO MUCH FURNITURE

Most of us have too much furniture. This is fine for living, but
not for selling. As you Stage, remove three or four big pieces
from your house. Living rooms and dining rooms usually contain too many chairs. Too many heavy pieces of furniture make
a room look and feel crowded to a buyer. Taking things away is
an important part of Staging. It opens up the house.

STAGE YOUR WALLS

In a room with lots of paintings or posters (in a child's room, for instance), take down all but one or two, patch the holes, and touch up the paint as necessary. Check the living room, family room, and even the baths for extraneous decorations on the wall. Take them down and pack them up early, to help get your house sold fast. We don't want to sell your paintings; we want to sell your house! Too many paintings constitute clutter and don't mean anything to a buyer. Put the extras away right now.

WHERE DO I STORE ALL THE STUFF I TOOK OUT OF MY HOUSE WHEN I STAGE?

- Throw it away (hardest to do, but highly recommended).
- Pack it away.
- Rent a storage unit or pod.
- Have a garage sale.
- Give it to charity.
- Put it in the attic.
- Stack it neatly in the garage.
- Store it in a protected crawl space.
- Use a corner of the basement.
- As a last resort, use a third or fourth bedroom as a storeroom.

COLOR

Every house has its good points, and color can bring them out. Painting is one of the least expensive ways to Stage your house. It's not always necessary, but it does make a home look better than the competition. Before you put your house on the market, consider painting the interior to simplify the colors. Navy blue bedrooms and wacky flower-print wallpaper may be fine when you're living there, but these kinds of rooms are hard to sell. When you Stage, each room should have a simple color scheme, and the whole house should be cohesive. Someone strolling from room to room shouldn't be startled by any of the colors.

If wall and carpet colors are intense or change from room to room, your house will seem smaller than it really is. The best wall color is so subtle that you may not even notice it, but something about the room just feels right. If your walls are in bad shape or the paint is an unappealing or distinctive color, repainting is a must. If hallways are marked or scarred, paint or wash the walls. Krud Kutter will get the marks off the walls without removing the paint.

I prefer walls that are fairly neutral. Taupe walls with white crown molding always look fresh. Odd neutrals like putty or moss also work, as long as the room has enough light—the brighter the room, the better odd neutrals look. Pick a safe color that works with the carpet and floor coverings in your home. I usually suggest off-white paint; there are many to choose from. Warm whites are more inviting than cool whites. Every paint color has a formula that includes a base color, and you can ask what the base color of a paint is before you buy it. Most paint companies now offer test samples the size of a coffee cup. What a great way to test out the paint on your walls! You can purchase several for about $5 each, paint them on the wall side by side, and see which looks best in the light in your house before you buy an entire can. I use the sample paints later for simple little projects that come up inside or outside my house, or in any house I am Staging.

Most furniture looks good against off-white walls, which makes it easy for a buyer to envision moving in. In all your rooms, create Staging's neutral backdrop. Then accessorize your rooms with a few carefully selected, colorful accessories, and an afghan, throw, or pillow. Never paint all the walls in your house strong, bright colors. Buyers only know what they see, not the way it's going to be. Too much color and the buyer will vibrate from wall to wall and leave the house. If you want to put some soft color on one wall of a room, that's enough.

REAL ESTATE BEIGE

Now, let's talk carpeting. You know what I'm going to say. Your carpeting shouldn't be purple, brown, wild yellow, shocking blue, black or white, shaggy, or patterned. I always recommend plain old real estate beige. Beige works well with most people's furnishings and should flow from room to room. Buyers respond to this expansive feeling. You won't get back the price of new carpet dollar for dollar, but buyers remember nice carpeting, and it's often the element that ultimately sells your house. If you don't replace worn carpet ("We'll let the

TIP

For Staging materials at minimal cost, Habitat for Humanity stores sell overflow items that weren't used and have been donated. To find out where the Habitat for Humanity store is in your area, look in your local phone book. I've found good buys on paint, wood, windows, and plumbing supplies there.

buyers replace it when they move in"), remember: Buyers only know what they see, not the way it's going to be. Most buyers have very little imagination. They won't be able to imagine a different carpet in the home. That's why I recommend buying new carpet yourself, instead of taking an allowance off the price of your house. Most buyers will keep looking for a house with fresh carpeting rather than going through the mental gymnastics of cutting a deal with you.

If you're not good about choosing paint or carpet colors, shop with a friend whose taste you admire. Better yet, go to StagedHomes.com and find an ASP to help you professionally.

WHAT BUYERS WANT

- Light, bright rooms
- Clean rooms
- Fresh, uncluttered rooms

I have trained ASPs in how to Stage a house and how to help you do it, too. Staging your house in the right plain and simple colors can do wonders to help sell your house.

You are selling your space. That is what buyers want, and that is what they will pay for. Staging your rooms will pay off for you.

Together, let's look at the individual rooms in your house. I'll show you how to Stage each one. We have just begun, and the secrets and the fun are ahead, especially for you.

CHAPTER 3

STAGING MAGIC: HOW TO STAGE EACH ROOM IN YOUR HOUSE

Now, we are ready to Stage the inside of your house. This really is the fun part! The way your home shows is one part of the sale that you can control. The living room, kitchen, and master bedroom are the three rooms buyers particularly focus on when they are looking for a house. But you should Stage every room for a perfect sale. I am always amused when sellers or agents tell me they want to Stage only a few rooms. I then ask, "Oh, you weren't planning on selling the whole house?" Then they laugh, too, and I end up Staging the whole house. You should do this as well. Let me show you how. (The chart on the next page compares the typical cost to improve various areas of a household and the resulting increase in sale price.)

A 2003 HomeGain survey of 2,000 real estate agents nationwide found that moderately priced home improvements, ranging from $80 to $2,800, made in preparation for sale, actually yield the highest returns when a house is sold. Here are the returns you can expect on various home improvements.

Your Return on Home Improvement Investments

Improvement	Typical Cost	Increase in Sale Price	Average Return	Agents Who Recommend
Lighten and brighten	$86–$110	$768–$935	769 percent	84 percent
Staging	$212–$1,089	$2,275–$2,841	169 percent	76 percent
Clean and declutter	$305–$339	$2093–$2378	594 percent	91 percent
Fix plumbing, electrical	$338–$381	$922–$1,208	196 percent	63 percent
Landscape and trim	$432–$506	$1,594–$1,839	266 percent	72 percent
Kitchen, bath upgrades	$1,546–$2,120	$3,823–$4,885	138 percent	83 percent
Repair flooring	$1,531–$1,714	$2,267–$2,589	50 percent	62 percent
Paint exterior walls	$2,188–$2,381	$2,907–$3,233	34 percent	57 percent
Replace carpeting	$2,602–$2,765	$3,585–$3,900	39 percent	65 percent

Data from 2003 HomeGain survey, at homegain.com.

HOW TO STAGE A ROOM IN 10 EASY STEPS

Here are 10 simple steps for Staging a room.

1. *Stand in the doorway.* This is where buyers stand before they decide to step into a room. If a buyer won't step into a room, he or she is not going to buy your house. You need to see what buyers see, so you can make the changes that will get them into every room of the house. Take a good look from the doorway to give yourself a buyer's point of view. Staging draws buyers into every room.

2. *Pick a Staging point.* This may sound like a fancy term, but it isn't. Just ask, "How will a buyer use this room?" If it's a bedroom, the Staging point is usually the bed. If it's a music room, the Staging point is probably the piano. In a living room, the Staging point could be the beautiful fireplace. Stage the room around this focal point.

3. *Make a plan.* Once you know what your focal point will be, make a plan to Stage the room. This plan isn't cast in stone; it's made to be changed. But a plan helps get you started. If you don't like the feeling of the room as you initiate your plan, change it.

4. *Clear the clutter.* Deaccessorize the entire room. Take out all the pictures, mirrors, and accessories. Put them in the hallway so you can see the "bones" of the room.

5. *Divide things into piles.* Pack, toss, give away, and sell. (Some things will go back into the room as you finish Staging.)

6. *Get rid of some of the furniture.* Or move it to another room. Is something crowding the room? Move it out! I often move a chair from the living room to the master bedroom, where it adds a cozy touch.

7. *Decide what furniture will stay.* Keep the basics; get rid of the extras—it's simple subtraction. Let's say a living room has a sofa, a love seat, two wing chairs, two barrel-shaped chairs, four end tables, one coffee table, and four table lamps. Here's how your thought process might go: First, you decide that the sofa and coffee table should stay; that makes sense. Then you decide to keep the wing chairs—another good choice. The love seat and barrel-shaped chairs are crowding the room—fine for living, but bad when Staging. Out they go! Without the love seat, you don't need two of the end tables or two of the lamps. The room looks much larger already.

8. *Arrange furniture the way you want it.* In the same room we were imagining, put the sofa in front of the fireplace, with a wing chair on either side of the fireplace. The coffee table goes in front of the sofa. Put an end table on either side of the sofa. Does it work? Yes! Less furniture, more space. The room looks open, balanced, and twice the size it did when you started. That's what Home Staging can do. Don't like the way it looks? Move things around again. There is no right and wrong. Work until the room looks spacious and open to you.

9. *Rebuild with accessories.* I love rebuilding a room with accessories from other rooms or finding a new use for

something—for example, making a curtain rod out of a golf club or an oar. Staging is all about creativity. When you bring accessories back into a room, remember that less is more.

10. *Fine-tune.* Stand in the doorway again. Is there anything else you can do? Anything else you can remove? Anything missing that needs to be added? Have you cut the tags off the pillows and throws? Are the blinds or shades hanging straight? Can you see any electrical cords (one of my pet peeves)? You get the idea. Take a long last look before you decide you are finished Staging the room.

Now let's go through your house room by room and see how you can Stage each of them to look their best.

THE LIVING ROOM

Buyers love a spacious living room. Clear off all the tables, including the coffee table. Then reaccessorize, using the Rule of Three or High, Medium, Low: Three items, or an odd number, is most pleasing to the eye. Leave just one or three magazines on the coffee table, or one nice vase or sculpture on a side table. Remove all ashtrays. Remove extra furniture and throw pillows (leave one or three); take stereo equipment off the floor; pack personal photos. Dried flowers and wreaths can look overdone and make a room seem smaller.

Do you really need the love seat and two chairs, or two love seats? Is an accent rug needed? How many ficus trees would

WRITE AN "AD" FOR YOUR HOUSE BEFORE YOU STAGE IT

To help you focus on your home's attractive features, describe them in writing. Write an ad for your home, imagining that you are seeing the property for the first time. In your mind, your home becomes a house, and then a product you want to sell.

One family wrote: "This home feels like a wonderful rustic retreat. It has an open floor plan, soaring ceilings, and a massive stone fireplace, and a wooded park-like setting."

Another family wrote: "This 1920s bungalow with original wood moldings is perfect for a small family. The kitchen is the heart of the house, with a center island for cooking and eating, and all-new stainless steel appliances. The finished basement is carpeted and includes a media center, which is included in the sale of the house."

With your ad in mind, Stage your house to play up the features that make it unique. When you Stage, feel free to relocate anything on your property. Sometimes outdoor things look even better inside (a rustic bench in a spacious master bath) or vice versa (a dining room bench moved outdoors). Be fluid when you Stage, and remain open to discovering new uses and different settings for things.

look nice? What additional greenery is needed? Are there bookcases? What will go in them? What artwork or mirrors are needed?

- Buyers will be impressed by space and light.
- Buyers will be disappointed by crowded rooms and spaces that feel too small. Crowded rooms lack energy. Staging brings back the energy when you declutter.

After ASP Staging

Staged to show
off the space.

37

THE KITCHEN

A sparse, clean kitchen looks bigger and helps a buyer mentally move in. A buyer considers the kitchen one of the most important rooms in the house. I know you feel the same way when you buy a house! Dishes in the sink, cluttered windowsills, and shelves packed with cookbooks cloud a buyer's vision. Anything you haven't used in three months can be put away or given away. What can you live without? Pretend you are camping. You wouldn't bring a grinder for the coffee beans, so grind extra coffee now, store it in the refrigerator, and put that grinder away while your house is on the market.

Most homes have too many small appliances out on the kitchen counters. Put them away, or give them away. And pack those kitchen collections, too, no matter how much you love them. Your antique plate collection, those clever mugs, the adorable salt-and-pepper shaker collection—gone, gone, gone! They distract the buyer's eye. You want to sell your kitchen space, not your collectibles.

Clear away all but one or three items from the windowsill. A small, healthy plant and a couple of knickknacks are all that's needed here—nothing else.

Repair tile or Formica countertops and edges that are damaged or have come unglued. If tile grout is stained, clean it with bleach. Remove liquor bottles and canisters. Replace them with a simple plate of green apples or a bowl of lemons, my favorite display fruits—bananas spoil too quickly.

Clean the stove top and oven. Replace burner pans if they are badly stained. Clean exhaust fans, filters, and hoods. Q-tip clean is required here; anything less just won't do. Pick up small scatter rugs; they make a room look smaller. If space allows, one large Asian rug in the middle of a kitchen makes a better statement. I like the look of a burgundy rug against a hardwood floor.

Empty the garbage regularly to prevent kitchen odors, replacing your wastebasket if necessary.

Move the dog and cat dishes, so buyers can't trip on them. Put them in a space that is out of the way and perhaps out of sight. I promise you your pets will find them. My "fur children" have no problem finding their bowls, no matter where I move them.

Now look at your refrigerator. If you're like most people, it's an exploding art gallery of photos, magnets, comics, and recipes, most of them past their prime. Throwing much of this in the garbage should be easy. I like refrigerators with nothing on them. Otherwise, choose one of your child's favorite drawings to display on the fridge and put everything else away. Anything truly necessary can be placed on the side of the refrigerator. Clean the top of the refrigerator, too, so it's spotless and clutter free.

Make sure kitchen windows and walls are clean. Paint the kitchen if it needs it; you'll get a great return on this small investment. Remove extra chairs from around the kitchen table and extra leaves from the table itself. We are selling your space, not the furniture. This makes the kitchen seem much bigger.

Scrub the refrigerator from top to bottom, inside and out (buyers will open it), and put a fresh box of baking soda in both the refrigerator and the freezer. Clear out extra food and condiments. I know a family who bought a house because the only thing inside the spotless refrigerator was a jug of chilled white wine, a wedge of Brie, and a plate of fresh strawberries—nothing else. It suited their fantasy of how they were going to live in the new house, and it helped make the sale.

Keep the kitchen sink clean and empty every day. Make sure the kitchen faucet is clean and works smoothly without drips. Stow soap dispensers, scouring pads, dish drainers, and paper towels under the sink. Clean and polish a stainless steel sink and faucet with double-zero-grade (fine) stainless steel and Krud Kutter.

Keep the whole kitchen neat as long as the house is on the market. This means every single day. You never know when the right agent and buyer will walk through the door. Keep your floor swept and spotless, too. You might even decide you like it that way all the time. I call that "living in a Staged home." Once you Stage to Sell, you will probably end up Staging to Live, too!

- Buyers will be impressed by a light, bright kitchen.
- Buyers will be disappointed by broken doors on the dishwasher, stove, or cabinets; missing hardware; leaking pipes or faucets; or a messy bulletin board or a refrigerator door brimming with notes.

PANTRY

A crowded pantry looks like there isn't enough storage room in the kitchen or in the house. Edit, organize, and Stage your pantry. Remove everything from the floor, including empty water jugs and bushel baskets. Wash the shelves. Stack products neatly on the shelves. Throw out everything that is not making the move or is not being used.

- Buyers will be impressed by a minimum amount of neatly arranged canned goods and bottled water.
- Buyers will be disappointed by bags of pet food and stacks of bottled drinks on the floor.

THE MASTER BEDROOM

The master bedroom is another room that really helps sell a house. Your goal is to break up the nest you've probably created here and Stage it anew for potential buyers. Put away all personal photos. Make the bed every day. Invest in a new bedspread; you can use it in your new home, and it isn't a huge investment. Clear tables and chests except for a few necessary items. Donate extra books and magazines, or store them out of sight under the bed. Play soft music on your clock radio at all times. Remove any dried floral arrangements. Pack away extra items on the shelves or in the bedroom wall units.

- Buyers will be impressed if the master bedroom looks open, airy, and romantic.
- Buyers will be disappointed if the room seems stuffy and overcrowded, with too much furniture. Open the windows whenever you can, so the air is fresh.

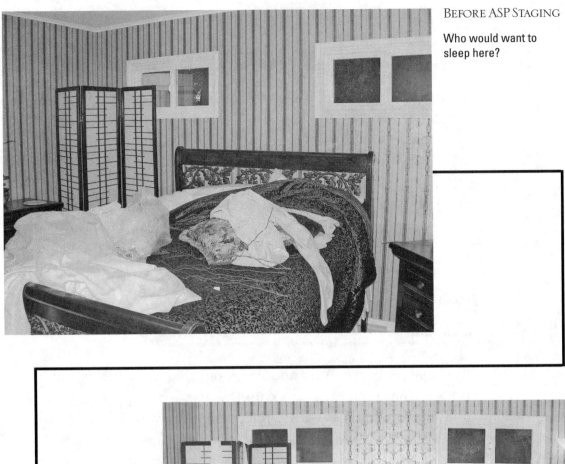

Before ASP Staging

Who would want to
sleep here?

After ASP Staging

A bedroom fit
for royalty.

42

After ASP Staging

Sweet dreams.

43

ALL BATHROOMS

In the bathrooms, cleanliness is crucial. Scrub them until they're immaculate: no scum, no mold. Counters, sinks, toilets, shower stalls, mirrors, and soap containers should all be sparkling clean. Remove extra rugs to showcase a nice tile floor.

Most bathrooms have too many things scattered on the counter, around the tub and shower, and on the back of the commode. Remove all unnecessary items. Put them in a cabinet or under the sink, or pack them up early.

Put away all but the most needed cosmetics, brushes, and perfumes, and tuck those into a basket, bowl, or tray.

Keep the lid down on the toilet and hide the wastebasket in a closet when your house is on the market. It may sound funny, but these two things subtly affect buyers when they look at a property. You are not marketing your toilet or your garbage. You want buyers to see the room, not your waste.

Use matching sets of towels, or coordinate them with the color of the room. If you don't have nice towels, buy some. You can display them in the bathrooms while the house is for sale and use them in the new house when you move. It's another small investment with a big payoff. Pretty towels are a visual cue that buyers remember and respond to. I always suggest that sellers tie their towels with ribbon, sisal, or rope. This discourages buyers from using the towels. Hide your own towel in another room. I like to Stage each towel with a silk flower or a piece of greenery slipped through the bow. It adds to that finished Staged look. In a boys' bathroom, I've tied plaid towels with bright neckties. Everyone loves it!

Check for any problems such as weak flooring where

bathwater has spilled. These things must be taken care of before the house goes on the market, and they must be disclosed in the listing agreement. Check the shower and tub for mildew, cracks, and dirty grout. Then fix them! Most bathrooms can benefit from a professional cleaning as well.

THE FOYER

Enhance the size of the foyer by keeping the area open and the floors clear. Remove all boxes and storage gear. Clear the hall table; I remove all candles and add some greenery or ivy to the table.

- Buyers will be impressed if the floors are clean and polished.
- Buyers will be disappointed by stacks of mail, piles of shoes, your baseball cap collection, and an overburdened coat tree. Move that stuff out. It pays off big-time!

THE FAMILY ROOM, DEN, BONUS ROOM, OR REC ROOM

Clear the family room as you did the living room. Remove everything from under the couch. Tie back the drapes to let in light, or take them down. The basement might be a better place for the big-screen television and stereo components while the house is on the market, so the room seems larger and less cluttered. Remove a chair, the record cabinet, the vacuum cleaner, your humorous Goofy telephone, sports posters—

Here's a great fireplace, but the furniture arrangement isn't showing it off to its best advantage.

After ASP Staging

Staged for cozy seating.

46

AFTER ASP STAGING

Now it's a
relaxing den.

everything that has piled up in here. I repeat: The way you live in your home and the way you sell your house are two different things.

- Buyers will be impressed with more space in the room.
- Buyers will be disappointed by darkness, clutter, and family photos of your daughter in the fourth grade. Put them away!

THE DINING ROOM

Make your dining room look as large as possible. A smaller table helps. If it has leaves, remove them and store them in a closet. Take at least two chairs to the garage or a storage unit; in most dining rooms, four chairs are plenty. The one exception is a huge dining room, when a large table is in proportion with the room's dimensions. Then use the leaves—buyers will be able to see that the room can handle a large table comfortably.

As in all rooms, remove extra items, expensive treasures, and collections. Edit the contents of your china cabinet so only a few simple pieces are displayed. Take any greenery off the top of cupboards and armoires; it can make the ceiling appear lower than it really is. Anything valuable should be packed away—this means most of your china and glassware, and all fragile items. Check that the lights in the chandelier are working, as well as the dimmer. You're creating coveted visual space.

Most buyers are looking for a formal dining room. Set the table and then stand in the doorway to make sure the room looks spacious.

- Buyers will be impressed if you set the table with chargers, china, and a nice centerpiece. (Don't use flatware; it is easily stolen.)
- Buyers will be disappointed if they must squeeze past a precarious Oriental vase on a pedestal or a man-eating flower arrangement.

CHILDREN'S ROOMS

Kids love to Stage. Once they understand what Staging is, they usually jump on the bandwagon and become enthusiastic participants. Show them my DVD *How to Stage Your Home to Sell for Top Dollar,* and they will become expert Stagers in no time. Kids can help pack or donate giant stuffed animals, most toys, and lots of clothes.

If there is more than one bed in a child's bedroom, consider removing one to open up the space. Flip a child's bedspread to make it look fresh or show a cleaner side. Putting the computer in the basement opens up the room. Repair nail holes, and paint the walls where posters have hung. If your teens have a fridge or a TV in their bedroom, move it elsewhere.

- Buyers will be impressed if the closets look roomy and the shelves aren't cluttered.
- Buyers will be disappointed if the walls are crowded with growth charts, kids' art, and posters of cartoon characters or celebrities.

BEFORE ASP STAGING

This kitchen area
has a cold feeling.

AFTER ASP STAGING

An orange tree, a
tablecloth, and
chargers and a bowl
of oranges on the
table make this corner
so much more inviting.

OTHER BEDROOMS

Set the Stage so these bedrooms feel like special guest rooms or deluxe hotel rooms. Roll the bedding back to show off the colors of the sheets and put a throw on the end of the bed. Open a book on the bed, and set up a bed tray with a cup and saucer and a rose in a vase.

On the housekeeping side, shampoo the carpet. Clean out the clutter. Dust, vacuum, and wash the windows and woodwork. Paint the walls a neutral color, no matter how much you like the bold color choice you've made. (Trust me on this.) To make a bedroom look larger, rearrange the furniture and consider moving furniture from one room to another. Make the beds with pretty sheets, shams, and a bed skirt and comforter, so the mattress doesn't show. I like bed-in-a-bag—those all-in-one sheets, comforter, shams, and bed skirt sets, which usually sell for less than $100. Believe me, setting the Stage in the bedrooms really pays off.

FORMERLY KNOWN AS THE GUEST ROOM

If your guest room has morphed into a sewing room or a storage room, return it to bedroom status. If you don't have an extra bed, use an inflatable AeroBed, dressed with sheets, quilt, and pillows, or my favorite, a camp bed with legs that folds up into its own carrying case when it's time to move. Follow the directions for Staging the other bedrooms, and make it as inviting as can be.

A guest room Staged with a special touch.

YOUR CLOSETS

Pack most of your clothes, so the closets look roomy. Edit mercilessly. Get your shoes off the floor! Get rid of the laundry and the clutter! Keep closet doors closed, but make sure the doors open freely without catching on the carpet.

- Buyers will be impressed if the closets are Staged with pretty hangers and lots of space, space, space!
- Buyers will be disappointed if opening a closet door triggers an avalanche.

A BEAUTIFUL HOTEL-STYLE BED CAN BE MADE FROM PRACTICALLY NOTHING

I needed to dress up an ordinary double bed, so I went looking around the house. In the linen closet I found some sheets and made the bed with lots of layers. I started with a fitted yellow sheet on the mattress, topped by a flat plaid sheet, a yellow flat sheet on top of that, finished with a white sheet brought halfway up and then rolled back, like a fancy, layered hotel bed. Then, on the floor of the garage, I found a cushion from an old webbed lounge chair. I pinned a sheet around it, nailed it to the wall above the bed horizontally, and covered each nail head with a glued-on button. Then I made bows out of raffia, and glued a bow to each button. Voila! Instant charming bed and headboard. Making something from practically nothing is one of the many fun parts of Home Staging.

THE LAUNDRY ROOM

Laundry rooms tend to be dark and gloomy, so I like to freshen them up. Make sure lightbulbs are working and bright. If there is a counter, add a small lamp set on a timer. It can be a fun-looking lamp that lends a sense of humor to the space, as well as adding needed light. Reduce the number of soaps and cleansers, and hide them in a cupboard or organize them neatly on a single shelf. Keep counters and sinks clean and empty. Never hang laundry when you're showing your house. Replace all wire hangers with matching white plastic hangers.

- Buyers will be impressed if your laundry room is fresh and inviting.
- Buyers will be disappointed if they're faced with your fine washables hanging right in front of them.

HALLWAYS

Remove plastic runners from carpets or hardwood floors. They are slippery and can be very dangerous. Keep the floors clean and clear. If the hall carpet is dirty, have it professionally cleaned. If it is in bad shape, replace it.

- Buyers will be impressed if the hallway walls are clean, the floors look great, and the marks or nicks in the walls are touched up.
- Buyers will be disappointed if they spot cobwebs in the corners of the ceiling or trip over your umbrella stand.

DO YOU HAVE A BASEMENT?

Properly Staged, the basement adds an extra room to your house. Make sure your basement looks large, cleared out, and full of potential. Repair cracks in the ceilings and the walls. Use dehumidifiers, disinfectant sprays, and absorbent agents to help remove odors and dampness. Open the windows for extra ventilation. Clean out the drains.

Make sure all light fixtures are working, and install new bulbs or fluorescent tubes to brighten up the space. Be sure the furnace, water heater, and sump pump are in good repair. Pack personal items. If you use the basement for storage, confine the boxes to one corner of the room.

- Buyers will be impressed if you create vignettes that show the basement's possibilities—for example, a poker corner with table and chairs, or a billiard room with a pool table cleared of anything that may have been piled on top.
- Buyers will be disappointed if the basement is damp, musty, shows signs of water damage, and is piled high with junk.

YOUR INSIDE-THE-HOME STAGING CHECKLIST SUMMARY

- Stand in the doorway of every room and look at it through the eyes of a buyer. What can you live without while your home is on the market?
- Replace worn carpet with a light-colored short plush or Berber carpet. Real estate beige is the safest color. At the very least, have carpets professionally cleaned or shampoo them yourself. This can still work wonders. Even spot cleaning the carpets is an improvement. Buyers only know what they see, not the way it's going to be.
- Make sure all light fixtures work properly. Replace burned-out bulbs and increase the wattage of bulbs, especially in dark hallways and corners.
- Repair and repaint cracks in walls and ceilings. Wash the walls with Krud Kutter and then patch the holes in the walls and touch up the paint—this is easy and adds a lot.
- Repair or replace broken light switches and switch plates, and clean the area around them.

- Keep curtains and blinds open during the day to let in light and views. The extra cost of additional heating or air-conditioning is a necessary investment when selling.
- Reduce the number of toss pillows on couches or sofas. Remove old or extra afghans and blankets.
- Pack up valuable items to protect them. When necessary, take them to a safe-deposit box.
- Take a hard look at your beloved houseplants. They usually need to be pruned or the number reduced to create more space. If plants don't look healthy or are just barely clinging to life, throw them away or give them to your best friend to house-sit while your house is on the market.
- Clean out your fireplace. Glass doors should be polished. Mantels and hearths should be cleared except for a few necessary items.
- To create more space, consider removing a chair, a love seat, or another large piece of furniture.
- Pack up all collections. They are a distraction from the desired focal point—your home.
- Reduce the number of books on the bookshelves. Pack them up or give them away.
- Remove family pictures from shelves, pianos, and tables. Buyers want to envision their family here, not yours.
- Reduce the number of wall-hung photos and paintings in every room to one large piece on a wall or a small group of three. Make sure they are hung at the average woman's eye level.
- Keep soft music playing at all times during showings. Choose an easy-listening station or light jazz, never hard rock or funeral music.

- If you can smell it, you can't sell it! Be sensitive to odors, because buyers are. Excessive cooking or smoking odors; dog or cat odors; and baby, laundry, and mildew odors will turn off buyers. If odors pose a challenge in your home, use room deodorants or disinfectant sprays and keep windows cracked open for ventilation, even in very hot or cold weather. Pet stores sell the latest products to tackle pet odors. An ozone machine can also help with difficult odors, but do have a professional handle this, as you and your pets and plants need to be out of the house for a day or two. This is a worthwhile investment when the odor is really bad and nothing else is working.
- Wash all windows and make sure they operate freely. If the seal on a double-pane window is broken, replace it now.
- Little things create clutter; pack up anything smaller than a football.
- Turn on lamps in all dark corners and make sure the bulbs are bright enough. You can put them on timers so they're on during key showing hours; this can save dollars, too.
- Repair anything that is broken. This shows that your home is well taken care of.
- Don't be afraid to move furniture from room to room. That extra chair from the living room or dining room may look great in the master bedroom.

Have fun as you Stage! When you make the sale, you'll be so glad you Staged.

CHAPTER 4

TAKE THE STAGING MAGIC OUTSIDE

Before you Stage the outside of your house, go safely across the street and view your property from a distance. Pretend you are the buyer and have never seen your house before. What do you see? Are the gutters coming loose? Is your yard in bad shape? Does the front door need repainting? Is the trellis past its prime? How long has that woodpile been stacked against the side of the house? You'll probably notice things you haven't seen for years. You must assess your house and property with an unemotional eye.

Buyers will be honest, even brutal, as they assess your house. They have no affection for your property until they fall in love with it and can imagine moving in.

Frankly, most of us don't even look at the outside of our house after we've bought it. We walk out in the morning, get in the car, and drive off to work without looking back. When we return home, we whisk into the garage without even seeing how our home really appears to outsiders.

But now you're selling. So cross the street and look back

over your shoulder. This is where an agent will park to tell prospective buyers about your house. What the buyers see determines whether they'll get out of the car or ask the agent to skip it and keep driving by. You probably know the expression "You never get a second chance to make a first impression!" That certainly applies here. You can't make buyers get out of the agent's car, but you can entice them by Staging. If the outside of your property isn't Staged, the buyer may think your property isn't worth seeing. They may say it looks too small, or seems overpriced, simply because the bushes have grown up over the windows or the property is obscured by too many trees.

Remember: You can't sell it if you can't see it! That saying of mine has made thousands of extra dollars for thousands of sellers. I remember the day I first said it. A client and I were looking at his overgrown property from across the street. His house had already been listed with another agent and expired off the market after sitting for three months. I explained to him that Staging the outside of his property was just as important as Staging the inside. You can't get buyers to see the inside if the outside isn't Staged, too.

If a buyer won't get out of the car, you never have a chance to sell your house. If peeling paint or an overgrown lawn discourages buyers, your property has just taken a giant step backward, no matter how good the house looks inside. So Stage your property inside and out. Whether your house is sitting on five acres or a small city lot, it still needs to be done. Stage every inch! Staging is merchandising, and merchandising the whole property is key.

Check the condition of the paint, roof, gutters, and downspouts. Trim the bushes and trees. Move garbage cans, discarded wood scraps, and leftover building materials. Check for termites, hornets, and other insect problems. Weed and mulch all planting areas. Groom and fertilize the lawn. Remove small items from patios and decks. Finish any unfinished projects, or realize they're not going to happen because . . . well, because you're moving. Let's get going!

THE STAGED HOUSE SOLD

The energy around your property says either Yes or No. Staging gives your property the positive energy and spirit it needs in order for it to sell. In a hot market, Staging will usually sell your house for more money. In a slow market, Staging will sell your house while other houses sit unsold. Staging doesn't mean you have to invest a lot of money. Staging means you'll use your creativity to find ways to Stage that are easy and fun, and that make sense. Sure, there are things you will invest in, but the creative ideas are the best investment of all, and they don't usually take much or any cash at all. The money you should focus on is the money you will receive by selling your Staged house. My motto? Keep it simple. Have fun, believe in yourself and your property, and proceed with a can-do attitude.

Your property has treasures that you have probably forgotten about or have hidden away—things you think aren't any good that can actually be used in wonderful ways to help you Stage your property. Always look in your garage—there are usually lots of good things in there. Empty garages are the only garages where I haven't found great things for Staging. Here are some Staging stories in which creative energy, ingenuity, persistence, and commitment made all the difference in getting the homes sold.

THE CASE OF THE MESSY NEIGHBOR

You can't change your neighbors; you can only work with the ones you have. We were Staging a lovely vacant house at the beach, but the neighbor's yard was a wreck: old car parts, overgrown grass, dead bushes, and no signs of life. One day I saw that someone was home, so I went over, introduced myself, and told him what we were doing (this can really make a difference). Turned out the messy neighbor was working in another city and wasn't home very often. When he found out what we needed, he cleaned up his yard a bit.

For our part, we built a wooden screen at one end of the beach-house deck that blocked the view of the messy neighbor's house, and brought in rental furniture arranged to show off the great view. Once we Staged the house—and talked with the neighbor—it sold, with five offers to choose from, after being on the market for almost a year. The Staged house sold.

THE CASE OF THE UGLY BROWN HOUSE

This was a classic case of a decent house that wouldn't sell because it looked so unappealing from the outside. The owners, a young couple, needed to move but said they had no money for Staging. However, I believe that all things are possible and it is up to us to figure out how to creatively make things happen. The couple had a garage sale and made $800, borrowed $300 from a friend, and invested it in getting their house sold. Here's how I suggested they invest the money.

The house had a long driveway. I advised them to rake it and add two loads of gravel. The seller worked with a man who was willing to build a short, curved retaining wall in front of the garden at the front of the house. I suggested they plant a row of my favorite trees, arborvitae. I asked them to build green shutters to hang on the front of the house and paint the garage door, which really needed it. The Staged house sold within a week, for $15,000 more than list price. They made the right decisions. They Staged, and it worked.

THE VACANT GRAY HOUSE

This sad gray house had been empty for three years. My suggestions completely changed the karma of the house. The sellers had laid new gravel in front of the house, but instead of leading to the house, it led the eye directly to a huge 60-by-80-foot barn that was big enough to build an airplane in. (I'm not kidding.) I recommended they hire some teens to rerake the gravel toward the house, not the barn. I encouraged them to add white shutters to the front of the house and paint the front door black. At the back of the house, we built a small landing outside the sliding glass doors, where previously there had been nothing but a drop-off—you had the feeling you would open the door, step outside, and maybe leap into the abyss. Do I need to say it again? Yes, you guessed it: This Staged house sold, and in record time.

NEW DIMENSION FOR A CLASSIC SPLIT-LEVEL

This typical split-level had been on the market for more than a year. The front of the house looked flat and uninteresting. To add a strong horizontal presence to the boxy facade, I asked a carpenter to build an arbor. It stood on tall, six-inch-by-six-inch posts above the front door and continued off to the right, above twin garage doors. We planted fast-growing honeysuckle vines to cover the arbor, and added a slate walkway to lead the eye—and buyers—directly to the front door. The Staged house sold. If the owners had Staged before they first put the house on the market, they could have probably moved earlier and saved all of those house payments. Staging first saves you time—and dollars!

THE HOUSE THAT WOULDN'T SELL

This concrete house could have won the ugly house award. It was cold and unappealing, and the owners confided that they didn't have enough money to invest in Staging. I asked whether they had any old paint in the garage to paint the facade, and they did. Then I recommended that they add lots of greenery in the front yard to warm up the cold feeling. How did we do that when they didn't have any extra money? Well, when the wife and I met at the nursery and she told me they couldn't afford the plants, we took another tack: I asked them to trans-plant plants from other parts of their yard to bring greenery to the front. It worked! The house took on a warm new look. The owner made a small, white, trellised arbor out of scrap lumber that was lying around in the backyard, left over from a deck they had built the year before. At my suggestion, they also made shutters to put on all the front windows. Although they hadn't received any offers before the Staging and the house had been on the market for a year, the Staged house sold in a week, at full price. In hot markets and even in slow ones, Staging works! Buyers only know what they see, not the way it's going to be. Please remember this saying of mine, and repeat it to yourself as you Stage your house.

A FORMULA FOR STAGING THE OUTSIDE OF YOUR PROPERTY

My favorite ways to Stage the outside of a house and garden are shutters, window boxes, "magic trees," a "Barb garden," general landscaping, and paint. Together, they have the power to dramatically transform your property.

Shutters

I love shutters and what they can do for a house. I put them on tiny bungalows; I put them on million-dollar homes. When I first look at a house, I always stand back, look at the windows, and ask, "Does this house need shutters?" Shutters can stretch the size of a window, and they are an inexpensive way to add class to any property.

I don't like the shutters with fixed slats that you find at most home centers and home improvement stores. Instead, I make my own shutters using one-by-fours, crossed with one-by-twos. You can make six pairs of shutters, paint them, and put them up for about $175. Now that is exciting to me—it's not a huge investment, yet it makes such a great statement.

Count the number of windows that need shutters, including windows on the back of the house, and even sliding glass doors. If you have a house on a corner lot, you will need to put shutters on the side windows, too. For each shutter, you'll need one-by-fours for the verticals and one-by-twos for the horizontal crossbars. For most windows, three one-by-four verticals and three one-by-two horizontals make a good-sized shutter. For a very wide window, use five vertical boards and three horizontals for each shutter. Have the lumberyard cut the one-by-fours to the height of your windows, measured top to bottom, including trim. Each one-by-two crossbar should be long enough to span the shutter side to side.

Lay the one-by-fours vertically on a piece of cardboard on the garage floor, spray them with primer, and then spray them black or white (sometimes I use slate blue or forest green; it depends on the color of your house). Hold the shutters together by nailing on three horizontal one-by-two crossbars. Attach the shutters to the house either by nailing them onto your house if it has wooden siding or with screws and molly bolts if you have a brick or stucco house. This is so easy, and you don't even have to have a saw because home improvement stores and lumberyards will usually cut them for you. Then all you have to do at your house is prime them, paint them, nail them together, and put them on your house. Look how great your windows and house look now! If you want to add even more character and charm to your house, add window boxes, too.

Window Boxes

A window box is like a smile beneath a window. Paint your window boxes the same color as your shutters. The idea is to keep the color going around the window, as though the window box and shutters were the mat around a picture you are framing. When window boxes and shutters don't match, the window looks like it has been chopped in half. Matching window boxes and shutters visually stretch the size of your house, giving it a larger, broader look. Choose a window box that's at least as high as a one-gallon container, making it easy to switch potted plants in and out.

Prime and paint the window boxes. Attach them to the house beneath the window, using brackets or screws. Attach them tightly, as window boxes can be heavy. Please do not use plastic window boxes. They just don't create the look you are seeking.

Fill the boxes with colorful geraniums, pansies, ornamental cabbages, or whatever is in season. Include ivy and trailing plants that cascade over the front of the box, and a few tall plants for height. Buy plants wherever you see fresh, lush, vigorous ones. I've even bought plants at the supermarket. You don't have to put a fortune into plants. Go to the garden section of your favorite store; I like the garden departments at Kmart, Wal-Mart, Target, Lowe's, and Home Depot. They have good buys and a great selection—and I'm there frequently anyway, shopping for other things.

Magic Trees

Greenery heals any property. One of my favorite secret weapons is those green pointed trees, big or little, that are shaped like oversized candle flames. They are called arborvitae, or emerald greens. I call them "magic trees" because they really do perform wonders wherever you put them. Magic trees can cost anywhere from $9.99 to $29 each if you shop around, or from $15 to $100 at a fancy nursery. These little guys look great in pots flanking your front door, or you can plant them right in the ground at the edge of your front porch where the sidewalk begins. A row of magic trees can help block traffic noise along the road or soften the look of a fence. Plant them closely for an instant hedge. I love magic trees and use them everywhere I can. A tip, though: Don't ask for "magic trees" at the nursery. The clerk will stare at you with incomprehension. Be sure to ask for emerald greens or arborvitae, and they will know what you want. Believe me, they really work. I have sold many houses that weren't moving just by suggesting that the owners buy and plant magic trees.

The Barb Garden: High, Medium, and Low

When you're Staging outside, freshen the garden, especially if your plantings are old, dying, or in need of new companions. Choose beautiful, healthy, lush-looking plants that show abundance. Buyers will see that you have a beautiful house for them to purchase. Green is a very prosperous color!

"High, medium, and low" is my formula for Staging a garden or any grouping inside or outside the house:

- For the high element, use a cedar, a fir, or my favorite, the clump vine maple, which has several trunks coming out of the ground and is very pleasing architecturally.
- The medium element can be a medium-size bush, such as a rhododendron.
- The low plants should be dense and green—like azaleas.

Plant the high, medium, and low plants in an easy arrangement at the end of your house, or centered where needed, but keep them in a casual grouping. I recommend putting trees and taller plants at the outer edge of your house, to visually stretch its size. Don't plant a tree in the middle of your yard; it cuts the house in half.

General Landscaping: Lawns, Shrubs, and Trees

Take a serious look at the outside of your property as a whole, as well as the landscaping (or lack of it). Landscaping has a major impact on a buyer. Is the tree you planted years ago now growing over the roof? Has the grape arbor gone from shady to sinister? Plants grow so fast that we sometimes don't notice how big they've gotten. Do the tough work now and trim them down. It's a quick way to attract a buyer. Your house looks better already!

You don't have to cut the entire plant down to the ground (although sometimes this is necessary). Most of the time, trimming some branches or doing some judicious pruning will do the trick. Trim all plants to below-window height so you can see the house and let light into the rooms. This shows off the view from the inside out. Trim plants from the top down. Trim trees from the bottom up (this is called "skirting the tree"). Trees and shrubs can frame a property beautifully, but unless they're tamed, they make your house appear dark inside. Light-filled homes are always in demand. Buyers always ask for light, bright houses that welcome them inside. If necessary, cut "windows" in a tree to show off a view or make it easier for the wind to blow through the branches. Most plants like to be trimmed; it's their haircut, encouraging them to produce more buds, grow larger, and if it's a flowering plant, flower more in years to come. Of course, dead plants or shrubs and all dying or dead foliage carry bad karma. Get them out of your yard.

Lush, green grass is inviting. I've been known to spray-paint my grass when my pets have left spots on it by veering off their graveled area. I know that sounds funny, but spray-painting my grass and my clients' grass has really worked. Someone said to me, "You kill the grass when you do that." And I responded, "The grass is already dead, so why not?" The grass does grow back even after you spray it green, and it looks great until it does. Some pet stores sell herbal-based (not steroidal) products for dogs so the urine doesn't burn the grass and turn it brown. Grass should be mowed every week during the growing season. Rake and weed the flower beds, and plant some cheerful flowers. They make a house look so appealing.

To sell your dirt, cover it! I like to mulch with finely ground brown bark. It seems to go well with the lush green plants, and it visually sets a Stage around them. If you live in a windy area, use the large ground bark so it won't blow away. I am a master gardener and I know that bark is discouraged for gardening, but now that you are selling your house and property, I encourage you to cover your dirt with some kind of ground cover. If you don't, you've got a picture (your house) without a frame.

In some parts of the country, crushed rock or gravel is the ground cover of choice. Use whatever is typical in your part of the world, but use something. A fresh layer of beauty bark, pine needles, gravel, or lava rock will put a finishing touch on your property. You can buy ground cover at all the home improvement stores; it comes in small, medium, and large versions.

Finally, edge your property: Edge the grass, the ivy, and the ground coverings around each plant. This really sells a property. Clean, crisp edges speak volumes about how your property is maintained.

Paint

What color is your house? It should be inviting, to welcome buyers to come inside. I always advise a soft neutral for the exterior of a house, such as white, cream, beige, light gray, or soft yellow. Painting your house a dark color like brown will only make it look smaller.

Make sure you choose a contemporary color by driving through neighborhoods where new homes are going up. Look at the color schemes that builders are using, and copy them if your house needs paint.

You can also get ideas at paint stores by examining the free charts and pamphlets filled with color ideas and color combinations. Some companies even offer page-size color picture cards, and, boy, do I love those! If you hold them to the wall, it's easy to imagine how a color is going to look. I like to keep these as reference for rooms I might paint in the future. Go to the store and head for the paint department to see what awaits you there.

Use no more than three colors on the outside of the house. For example, if your house is light gray (one of my favorites), try white shutters, white trim, and a black or burgundy front door.

Paint the whole house if you need to improve the color or the condition of the paint. If your budget won't permit that, just paint the front door, the trim, the downspouts, and the shutters.

By the way, the cost of painting a house is in the labor, not the paint. So, if need be, ask your neighbors, friends, and

GOOD NEWS: LOOK WHAT ONE GALLON CAN DO FOR YOU!

A gallon of paint, on sale at the hardware store, can cost less than a pack of cigarettes or even that caffé mocha these days. And that gallon can work miracles when you Stage.

One gallon can give a crisp new look to hundreds of items and places, including

- Trim.
- Front door.
- Shutters.
- Window boxes.
- Child's room.
- Small bath.
- Outdoor furniture.
- Planters.
- Wooden wagon.
- Several flowerpots.
- Wheelbarrow.
- Garden gate.

relatives to pitch in. Announce a paint party, offer to feed them beer and barbecue, and they'll usually show up. Paint is cheap in comparison to the return on that investment!

OUTDOOR CHECKLIST

When you're Staging your home's exterior, focus on the following areas. Completing these steps will help you sell your house for more money, no matter what the market is doing.

Front Door

To make your house look crisp and in good condition, paint or stain the front door. It's the entry to your house—and to the buyer's new home. It's also one of the least expensive ways to dress up a house. At the front door, buyers will get a first impression of your house and have an opportunity to make a close inspection. I usually recommend red, black, or dark green for the front door. But don't be afraid to break the rules. I know a homeowner who painted her front door a rich berry pink and surrounded it with cement urns overflowing with fresh pink petunias. Everyone said it was too much, but the home sold within two weeks of being listed, and the buyer said it all began when she saw that bright pink door—her favorite color!

Front Entrance

Add color by your front door. Plant small flowers around the base of emerald green trees in pots on either side of the door. Remove ornamental lions, frogs, and bunnies. These are usually

too much for the buyer's eyes to process. We want them to con-
centrate on the house, not on all the little figurines outside. (I do
love those bunnies, but not when you are selling!) Remove any
large evergreen, bush, or tree that crowds the entry and hides
the doorway from the street. Be sure all holiday lights and icicle
lights are removed from the shrubbery and trim.

Roof

The roof and gutters should be free of debris and moss. Trim
branches around the roofline to keep animals, insects, and
foliage off the roof.

Fences

Fences should be in good repair. Fix and paint them if necessary, or whitewash them if that is more appropriate.

Decks, Porches, and Patios

Sometimes the smallest improvements can make a big difference
in the way your house shows. Power-wash, stain, or paint your
decks, porches, and patios as necessary, to remove dirt, moss,
and mildew. Sweep them every day. Reduce clutter to create the
impression of space. Get rid of old flowerpots, barbecue grills,
charcoal, planters, toys, construction materials, and excess furniture. If you have outdoor furniture, Stage an inviting seating
area—an outdoor room—around a table or fire pit, so buyers
can see how useful the space is. Outdoor rooms really do appeal
to today's buyers, and that is what Staging is all about.

Store sports equipment and extra furniture out of sight, in a
storage unit, the garage, or the basement. Remove tumbledown
swings, gliders, and that extra or older grill. Children's toys

should be weeded out, cleaned, and organized in just one small area of the backyard or put away entirely. Throw away that abandoned sandbox. Stage to show off your spacious yard and property, just as you've done indoors. The same principles apply.

Driveways, Walkways, and Sidewalks

Paved driveways should be cleaned and swept and oil stains removed or reduced with a product especially designed for that purpose. Once again, Krud Kutter comes to the rescue. Repair the driveway to fix cracks where needed also. If you have a basketball hoop, be sure it's in good condition. If the net is torn or missing, replace it or take it down. Gravel driveways should be freshly raked, weeded, and rerocked as necessary, for a fresh, full look.

- Buyers will be impressed when your driveways, walkways, and sidewalks are swept and clean. After all, this is the runway to the inside of your house. You want people to feel uplifted when they get out of the agent's car and start to walk toward your home—just as fashion designers set the Stage with a beautiful runway.
- Buyers will be disappointed if they must shuffle through fallen leaves or snow, trip on a broken sidewalk, or mistakenly step in dog-doo, mud, or matted clumps of cut grass.

Garage or Carport

Carports have to be cleaned out completely—everything must go! Discard it, or pack it up and hide it. Garages should be swept and organized. If you have to use part of or the entire garage for storage, that's fine—just keep it neat. Keep the workbench area of your garage uncluttered and clean so that buyers can imagine working there when they move in.

Always keep garage doors closed when your home is on the market. If you're not using the garage for storage, keep cars in the garage, not in the driveway.

Move boats, trailers, and recreational vehicles to a storage facility or a neighbor's home several doors away until your house sells. (If you don't, buyers might try to buy your RV instead of your home.)

- Buyers will be impressed if your garage is clean, neat, and organized. Make sure a side door or other entrance isn't blocked. Replace burned-out lightbulbs and add more if you need to, so the garage has enough light. It is worth it. You can't sell the garage if you can't see it.

- Buyers will be disappointed if your garage is brimming with tools, old paint cans, and flowerpots, or if it has a funny smell. Some garages smell like an oil factory, and that sends buyers running. Set the Stage in the garage.

If you can't sell your house, cut the shrubbery! *If someone says your house is overpriced,* trim the bushes! *When a real estate agent tells a fellow agent that one of her listings is overpriced,* skirt the trees! When buyers can't see your house, they don't stop by. If they do take a look, they think your house is smaller than it really is, or that it's overpriced. So get out the hedge trimmers, cut those branches, sell your house, and get the money your property is really worth!

HOPE AND GUILT

"I don't think this one is going to make the move." That's what I say whenever I find something in someone's house that's clearly about to croak (or already has). It could be a desperate ghost of a palm tree that has lost its verve, a houseplant that has withered, or a broken-down piece of furniture that should have been trashed long ago. I'm gentle when I make these observations, but the joke usually makes homeowners smile, and they realize I'm right. Then I help them carry the item to the trash. We all hold on to things because we hope they'll come back to life or we'll find a new use for them (this usually doesn't happen). Or we feel guilty if we toss them. So I am giving you permission to let go in this case. Let go of the guilt. If you still can't throw something away, give the item to a friend or ask them to dispose of it for you. Your job is to get that thing out of *your* house. You're Staging!

"Hope and Guilt" Plants

Poinsettia out of season.
Sad pine tree that never flourished.
Plant with all its leaves gone.
Plant with leggy growth that is taking over the inside or the outside of the house.
Last year's flowers that didn't grow back.
Weeds that you think just might be real flowers.
Pots of dead plants on a deck or patio.
Dead or expiring plants in the garden.

    The list goes on and on, but you get the idea. If in doubt, toss it out. If it was worth keeping, you wouldn't have had the question in the first place.

Continued

"Hope and Guilt" Stuff

Old barbecue equipment.

Dilapidated outdoor furniture.

Old cans and bottles.

Old tools (not antiques, but not in good repair).

Broken toys.

Aquarium (give to a neighbor or friend).

Abandoned fish pond full of algae (either clean it out and make it nicer, or fill it in).

Old doghouse and padding inside.

Cement blocks that are just sitting around.

Scraps of unused lumber.

Awnings and outdoor gazebo that aren't in good repair.

Broken pumps or other equipment.

Work shoes around outside doors.

Broken railings front or back—get rid of them and put in new ones.

Move It, Hide It, Toss It Out

Piles of lumber or decaying firewood.

Auto parts.

Old windows.

Newspapers.

Piles of grass or kindling.

Empty cans.

Old window boxes.

Extra flowerpots.

Those plastic plant markers.

If you haven't used it in a year, toss it out. Why would you pay to take that stuff with you, when you haven't used it? That's a good question to ask of everything, inside or outside. Stage to Sell, and it will become a way of life.

CHAPTER 5

GETTING IT DONE: IT'S COMMITMENT TIME

At this point you may be thinking, "This is a lot to do—how can I get it all done?" Well, first of all, you probably don't have to do all of the things that I have talked about in just one house (or do you?). So your list probably isn't going to be as long as these chapters are (I hope!). Although I have seen the worst of the worst and the best of the best, I promise you, you can do it. In the movie *Jerry Maguire,* the character played by actor Tom Cruise said, "Show me the money!" That is what this is about for you, too. Let's get you the money from the sale of your house.

I have a saying on my wall: "A journey of a thousand miles begins with a single step." You don't need to walk a thousand miles to Stage your house. It's much easier than that. Step by step, one thing at a time, it is amazing how fast you can Stage your house. It is work, yes, but it is fun, too—and I must say, it is addictive. Staging works, and you feel good as you make progress. Once you begin, you will find you simply cannot stop.

Let's face it: When you live in a house, you tend to let things go. That's because you live there. You probably have a list in your head of Things I Need to Get Around To that never seems to get any shorter. Well, now you have a great reason to get around to them: You want to sell your house and get more money for it. Staging is how you are going to accomplish that.

Now that it's time to start Staging, you may also be thinking, "These ideas are great, but I'm starting to feel overwhelmed. I don't have time to do this. This could cost too much. Let's just try to sell the house the way it is and see what happens." I ask you, "Do you want to 'try' to sell your house, or actually get the job done?" Yoda, in *Star Wars*, said, "Do or do not. There is no try." I feel the same way. If you want to sell your house and get top dollar in the shortest amount of time, you need to Stage. Get behind the idea and do the job right. If you don't have the time, log on to www.StagedHomes.com and find an ASP to help you. It's also worth taking a day or two off work to Stage your home, because for most of us, two days' pay is far less than you will make by Staging and selling your home.

Staging your house will put extra dollars in your pocket. Our statistical information here at StagedHomes.com shows that Staged homes nationally are selling for anywhere from 10 percent to 20 percent more than homes that are not Staged— and many are selling for much more than that. This includes houses from Little Rock to San Francisco, from New York to Los Angeles. The selling price of your home could be $20,000, $50,000, or even $100,000 more than if you hadn't Staged. I haven't seen this just a few times; I've seen it happen hundreds and thousands of times. Simply put, Home Staging works.

TAKE A DEEP BREATH

Most people start Staging with one to three pages of things to do. The list can seem impossibly long, but your home will show better for the effort you've put in. Your list might look something like this:

- Move recliner from family room to garage
- Paint front door trim
- Fix broken dishwasher
- Replace missing handles or knobs on cabinets or appliances
- Throw away old lumber in the garage

Deal with each task individually, one by one. When your list is complete, you are going to feel so good about your house and about yourself. That feeling will take you all the way to the bank.

Remember, if you have to reduce your list price because you didn't Stage your home, you will lose thousands of dollars. One of the most accurate sayings I've come up with about Home Staging is "The investment in Staging your home is less than your first price reduction." That is the solid truth. Having a garage sale will put a little bit of money in your pocket, but Staging brings a far greater return. Why not do the thing that makes you the most money? If you don't Stage your house, you are cheating yourself. Don't leave money on the table. Stage your house.

LOOK TO THE FUTURE

Why are you moving? Do you need a bigger house because a baby is on the way? Have you been transferred? Are you getting divorced? Envision your new life and hold it as your focus as you move ahead. You are earning your equity by Staging your house. It is sweat equity, but it doesn't take that long, and the payoff can be huge.

You learned the importance of clean, clutter, and color in Chapter 2. The remaining steps—commitment, compromise, creativity, and communication—will complete your Staging tasks. Together, they are the all-important Seven C's of Staging.

COMMITMENT

Everyone involved must be committed for Staging to happen. If you're doing the Staging yourself, you must be committed to Home Staging. If you're working with an ASP real estate agent (and I hope you are), he or she will be committed to help you along the way. And if you're getting help from an ASP Stager, he or she will be committed to the whole Staging process. Both an ASP Stager and an ASP real estate agent already know the difference that Home Staging makes. All parties need to be committed to the results.

Set a deadline for getting your property Staged. Make a commitment and stick to it. Be accountable to that commitment. Commitment and accountability are crucial in getting a house Staged. My clients through the years have always made the commitment, and together we have been accountable for making it happen. Each of us contributes our respective part of the commitment to get the desired result. I think my job is to help my clients set the deadline, hold them accountable, and praise them as they keep that commitment. This way, we all work together in a positive way and, wow, does it pay off! Commitment works—you know in your heart when and if you are committed. So set your deadline, make your commitment, and hold yourself accountable. Get your family on board and, together, be the team that makes it happen.

Make a "Do" Date

Set a deadline for completing your Staging, and note it on your calendar, in your PDA, or on a pad of paper on a clipboard. Your agent should have figured Staging into the equation when deciding on a suggested list price for your home; the list price and the selling price depend on the Staging being complete. Ask your agent whether he or she is an ASP real estate agent. To find out more about the ASP designation, read Chapter 9.

I encourage you to do all your Staging tasks right now—ask friends to help if you must—rather than going back to a project later. It's human nature to procrastinate, so finish Staging as soon as possible, before you lose steam. Anything that can't be done immediately should be assigned a "do" date and checked off as it is finished. The "Staging Criteria" in the "Staging Resource Center" in the back of this book can help. When every box on the list is checked off, you have a Staged home. Be your own taskmaster. Your house will be Staged and ready to hit the market sooner, and it will look better than the competition. That means a faster sell—and, usually, more money.

If you start to show your house before everything is packed up, painted, and put away, inside and out, you won't get as large a payoff. Remember, buyers know only what they see, not the way it's going to be. Staging your house is in your best interest. If you want to sell, Staging is the best and fastest way to do so. Even if no one ever paid you to do your homework in the past, this time they will. Finishing the Staging doesn't have to mean spending a lot of money, but you will invest time and energy. If your to-do list takes a weekend to complete, think of it as an investment you're making to earn a monetary reward in the end.

COMPROMISE

Life is a compromise in many situations, isn't it? Well, Staging is a compromise, too. Let me give you an example: Let's say your kitchen floor is black, white, and gray vinyl, and has a few tears in it. It looks very worn. The primary bathroom has pink tile. It's in good condition but looks dated. Imagine you have enough money to invest in replacing one of them, but not both. This is where the compromise comes in. You are going to replace the one that will give you the highest rate of return and the best overall look to sell your property.

Answer: Replacing the kitchen floor should be your first order of business. Put the money there for the best look. Now, for the bath with the pink tile, let's compromise. We'll Stage it by going retro. Let's bring in a big basket and place black towels inside the basket. Let's tie the towels in the basket with black-and-white checked ribbon for a crisp, fresh look. Keep the shower curtain simple, without a pattern; I've purchased white cotton and white chenille shower curtains at Target that look good and don't cost much. You could also tie the shower curtain onto the shower rod with the black-and-white checked ribbon, which will look terrific and go with the towels. How much better is that than just plastic shower rings? Much better, I say. Now, clear all the little perfume bottles, shaving cream cans, hairbrushes, and mirrors off the counter and put them in a cupboard or hall closet. Put the big basket containing the towels on the counter, and you have finished Staging the room. To create the biggest impact, we replaced the kitchen floor and jazzed up the bathroom, and now both look great. This is what I call a real win-win situation. We compromised, and it worked.

USE YOUR CREATIVITY

Staging takes more creativity than money, and creativity is the mother of Home Staging. Creativity is alive in you—yes, it is. In fact, it is one of my very favorite parts of Staging. Many people say they are not creative. If you are one of them, stop saying it now. What you say is what you create in your life. Start saying, "Wow, I am so creative." If you don't believe it, then pretend. All kinds of research has been done on this point, and it is true. Fake it until you make it come true. This really works. I used to tell myself that I was not creative, and lack of creativity is what showed up. When I stopped doing that, things got better and better. The more I compliment myself quietly, the stronger my creativity becomes. See, your body is creating right now. Your heart is creating life by keeping the blood flowing, and your mind is similarly creating all kinds of thoughts as you read this book. It is either agreeing with me or not, and there's probably a part of you that's saying, "Well, yeah, I am creative in some areas, but not in this one." I say to you, let it flow and believe in yourself. Just by thinking, you are being creative. A snapshot of a bedroom staged with creativity is shown below.

Go outside and cut some flowers, or buy some. Then arrange them, step back, and say, "It worked"—no matter how they look. You have to start somewhere. Paint a wall. You can do it. Then go to your garage, grab a fishing pole, and hang it above the window as a curtain rod in a child's room or your

Kraft paper and a "fence" made of twigs transformed a white wicker headboard. Dad's shirts were stuffed with bed pillows tied with belts. Twigs spell "Dream" on paper-covered cardboard. Now that's creativity!

den. Drape a sheet over the rod, swag it to one side, and tie it back to the wall with some rope. You've created something! A few long nails in the wall above the window will hold up the rod. It doesn't have to stay there forever, but it's so much more imaginative than going to the store and just buying a plain old curtain rod. You could also use a baseball bat, or a golf club, or a long branch clipped from a maple tree. I have done similar things many times, and they all looked great. Think outside the box and make it happen. Creativity doesn't belong in a box. It needs to be free to do its thing.

Anyone can buy furniture, but how creative is that? If you need some more furniture, buy some, of course, but you probably have enough furniture already—most of us have too much. You may just need to rearrange it and move some pieces to other rooms. Play with it. Have fun. The results will encourage you to do more. Use your creativity and be thankful for it; this allows more creativity to flow through you. Have confidence in yourself. If you don't, no one else will. When you tap into your creativity, you'll Stage a look that buyers can respond to.

In the ASP courses that I offer, I like to put the tempo and temperature of the room at the "creativity" setting. No negative talk is allowed. Only positive words are spoken. Compliments are freely given, and we begin to believe in ourselves and each other all the more. Try this in your family life: Surround yourself with those who believe in you, and play with the creative side of life. Being bored is a sad state. There is no need for it when we have the gift God gave us called creativity.

COMMUNICATION

Communication is very important when you Stage—especially the communication you conduct with yourself. You talk to yourself more than to anyone else. I believe that the way we talk to others is a reflection of how we talk to ourselves. The most important person to communicate with in Home Staging is *you*. Tell yourself, "I can do this." Then tell your spouse, your significant other, your roommate, your kids, and your friends and associates. Don't get in your own way when you Stage, and don't let others get in your way, either. Keep your self-talk positive.

THE RULE OF THREE

I love the number three. As I've mentioned, it shows up in Home Staging all the time. Three items look pleasing to the eye. Put three things on a coffee table. Group three pictures on a wall. You don't have to strip the house bare, but limit groups of small objects to one, three, or five; the odd number always works. If you have 15 little Hummel figures you've collected over the years, pack most of them, and display only one or three. Stack magazines that are scattered on the coffee table in the living room, but don't leave out any more than three. Remove extra pillows, afghans, candles, clocks, newspapers, and pet paraphernalia from every room. Clear off the mantels, leaving only a simple arrangement of one, three, or five things. Often, on a mantel, one large mirror or painting is the most impressive.

High, medium, and low is a variation on the Rule of Three. As I've mentioned, use the high, medium, and low principle when you set things on a coffee table, position pillows on a sofa, or place candles on a table. When you plant a garden, put in three plants, or just one, but never two or four.

SNAPSHOTS

Before you Stage, take pictures of your house during the day, inside and out. What the camera sees and what you see are two different things. The pictures will help you view your house with an unbiased eye. Overlooked trouble spots are glaringly apparent in a photograph: piles of mail, a sooty fireplace, a tired bathroom, the old compost heap, your falling-down dog-house, and the wisteria blocking the front porch. Look through the viewfinder and let the camera lead your eye (but be careful not to walk off the edge of a floor into a sunken living room or fall down steps, as I have!). When you see a good picture, click. Refer to your photos to determine what needs to be Staged. You'll look back on them later as great "before" shots.

THE MARKET'S SO HOT, I DON'T NEED TO STAGE

Sometimes I meet homeowners and real estate agents who tell me there's no need to Stage a house when everything that comes on the market sells so quickly. I always reply, "Can a house ever sell for too much?" Regardless of what the market is doing, Staging will sell a property faster and usually for more money.

In a hot market, if it's going to sell anyway, why not Stage it so that it will sell for more money? In slow markets, homes that are Staged may not sell for more money, but they usually sell faster than other homes on the market that are not Staged. While a house sits on the market, you're still paying the mortgage, and if you have to reduce the price of your house, your profits are correspondingly reduced. So whether the market is active or slow, whether it is hot or not, you will get top dollar for your house if you Stage. In any market, Home Staging works.

CHAPTER 6
STAGING ON A DIME

Ilove making things out of nothing. I look at the world differently, and I ask you to do the same. Staging doesn't mean spending a lot of money. With a ball of rope and a pair of clippers, you can Stage your house using the simplest things. At one of my seminars, an ASP found a huge tree branch with otherworldly orange blossoms on it and brought it to a house we were Staging. It became a standout focal point on top of a glass table in the backyard—and it cost nothing, nothing at all. Keep your eyes open and your antennae out. Some of Staging's best props can be found curbside on trash day; at garage sales, close-out sales, and discount stores; or as giveaways from relatives.

My signature item is raffia. In my opinion, raffia is to a woman what duct tape is to a man. It comes in colors, too. I use raffia to make napkin rings, wrap flowerpots, and bind decorative sticks in a large vase. (I also tie raffia around the decorative towels on display in a Staged home, to discourage buyers and agents from wiping their hands on them!) I've Staged a headboard for a child's bed by nailing animal-shaped paper plates to the wall (more on that later) and filled wine goblets with glitter and votives, all for pennies.

Staging involves using things in new ways and seeing possibilities. Ask "What do I already have that I can use? What else could I do with this?" Some of the best Staging materials are everyday things you probably have in the house. Here are some of my favorite items for Staging and ideas for how to use them:

- King-size flat sheets in white, beige, or cream. Drape them over tables for that *House & Garden* look. Hang them as curtains, using clip-on rings, or just swing them up and over the rod, twisting and tying until they look right. I love making drapes without sewing a single stitch. Long lengths of fabric can be used the same way.
- Tapestries, throws, scarves, and sarongs. Use them as table toppers. Cut a long tapestry in half to get twice the use out of it. Or trim a square of 54-inch fabric with sewn-on or glued-on fringe. I recently discovered a product called Zips, which are little glue dots that unroll from a spool—like having a glue gun without the gun! These are great for quick, no-sew projects.
- White plastic tables, 36 inches or 48 inches in diameter. These lightweight backyard tables can be used in a kitchen, dining room, or anywhere you need a table. If your regular table is too big, replace it with one of these to make the room look larger. (Remember, you're not selling the table, you're selling the room.) Cover it with a tablecloth or a king-size sheet and use a table topper for a more dramatic effect.
- White plastic chairs. Buy tie-on fabric slipcovers to dress them up. These look great around a kitchen table, for a garden look indoors.

BEFORE ASP STAGING

This old chair was
showing its age . . .

AFTER ASP STAGING

. . . so we took down a
heavy master bedroom
drapery and used it as
an ingenious slipcover.
What a great idea!

- Small wooden folding chairs. Same deal as the white plastic chairs. Cover with tie-on fabric slipcovers, or you can make a quick slipcover by draping a chair with a sheet, knotting all four corners at the floor, and tying a knot to each chair leg using rope. This sets the Stage in an inexpensive way. A pair of small wooden chairs and an accompanying side table can be used anywhere, often adding just the right extra touch.

- Towels. Buy several sets in different colors; they're an investment you can take with you. My favorite towels are black. They make low-end homes look classier and befit the high-end homes. For a children's bath, use one or two bright colors, like yellow and orange, and for whimsy, prop a shiny green plastic frog behind the towel bar, looking out into the room.

- Metalwork—lanterns, bowls, open-weave baskets, mirrors, and candleholders. I use a lot of metalwork when I Stage. It adds weight and substance to any room.

- Weeds, branches, grasses, and dried flowers, much of it from your own backyard. When I trim my yard I always set aside some cuttings for Staging. I like bringing the outside in. If you live in the city, bring cuttings back from your weekends in the country.

- A can of buttons. You never know when you might need a button! I use them to cover nails when I hang something up, and for decorative touches everywhere, as the mood strikes.

- Silk greenery and plants, especially orchids. (I use a lot of these.) These days, silk orchids look so real—sometimes even better than the real ones! I love real orchids, but in

Staged homes I often put in the silk ones because they need no care at all. Discount and import stores sell silk plants and vines at affordable prices.

- Dried flower arrangements. Buy these at bargain prices, or make them yourself.

- Baskets, all sizes. Accessorize with large baskets; they have the most impact. Smaller ones can be used to contain things that tend to get strewn all over a room.

- Decorating magazines with thick, attractive covers. *Architectural Digest, Veranda,* and *Southern Accents* are my favorites. Stack them on an entry table, or in the living room on a coffee table, bench, or small table.

- Area rugs. Use these judiciously. You don't want to cover up beautiful hardwood floors or make a room look smaller. As a rule, use fewer rugs when you're Staging than you would if you were living in a house. For Home Staging, a great rug placed at an angle under a table or sofa is wonderful, and just enough.

- Trees are great for Staging. They add another dimension to a room, and greenery is always healing. For the most impact, any tree you use should be large and healthy, set in a huge pot. Silk ficus trees are okay, too; they come in all sizes at all prices. Beware of sickly plants. There's nothing worse in a room than a sick, leggy plant. That kind of plant sends the wrong message—it says, "I am poor and no one wants me," and that rubs off on the house, too. Ruthlessly assess your plants. Only the lush, healthy ones should stay.

- Large-scale knickknacks. Even though they're large, don't use too many of them. Small items get lost in a room;

please put those away. It's much better to choose one big, bold "something" to anchor a room. Remember, clutter eats equity. Large items are always better than small ones when you are Staging.

- Large bath rugs. One big bath rug makes a statement; scatter rugs look ditsy. And get rid of all those fluffy rugs—fluffy doesn't live here anymore. For bathrooms, I always suggest a large faux-Asian rug with a rubber backing. It's slip-proof and has a great look. You'll pay about $15 for a rug like this.

- Lamps of all sizes. These are invaluable for Staging. Floor lamps are especially useful, as they don't need a table to stand on. Look for fun lampshades, change the shade, or cover one yourself with paper or fabric for a custom look.

- Light is so important when you're selling a house—I can't emphasize that enough. People don't want to live in dark houses. Put your lamps on timers whether you're Staging to Sell or Staging to Live. In either case, you'll come home to a cheerful, bright home, and save dollars, too.

- Ribbon, grass rope, twine, and anything creative to tie around towels and bouquets.

- Mirrors, wall art, and pictures. Large ones have the most impact. Discount shops offer these at very reasonable prices. I usually invest between $50 and $60 for a large picture. You shouldn't have to invest more than $100.

- One radio for every level of the house, all tuned to the same soft-music station.

- Plant stands made of wire, wicker, or wood, as focal points in a hallway, entryway, living room, or dining room.

- Wicker furniture, in all sizes, styles, and colors. It is light and easy to carry. I look for unusual pieces, and frequently rely on wicker for a fix in family rooms and master suites, and on porches.
- Afghans, all sizes, shapes, and colors, with fringe and without. Use them on sofas and chairs in the usual way, or as wall art, as window coverings, on tables, on a hanger as a pretend dress—let your creativity flow.
- Pillows! Bed pillows, accessory pillows, neck rolls, European squares—all colors, styles, and sizes. These are Staging must-haves!
- Dishes, glasses, napkins, place mats, napkin rings, chargers, in several colors and styles.
- Inflatable camping beds, twin-size and queen-size. They come on a frame so they're off the floor. Find them in the camping department (not the bedding department) of large big-box retailers. I have not seen king-size, and that's fine with me, because the queen-size makes bedrooms look larger. Don't forget a pump to blow up the inflatable camping beds.
- Beds-in-a-bag. I always buy king-size because the sheets can be folded, pinned, and tucked to fit any size bed, table, or window.

THE HAVE-TO-HAVE-IT TEST

If you're shopping and see something you really love but it's not on your Staging list or in your Staging budget, do what I do:

Put it in your cart, keep shopping, and when it's time to check out, see if it passes the have-to-have-it test. Do you have to bring it home or can you just enjoy it here at the store? If something doesn't pass my test I put it back, no matter what it is or what the price is. Often, by the time I get to the checkout my excitement has diminished and I can happily leave the store without the item, leaving me the richer. Only things that pass my test go home with me. I ask my intuition and it tells me whether I really need it or not. This little test has saved me money time and time again.

ESSENTIAL STAGING TOOLS

I carry a tote with me when I Stage, filled with handy little tools. Gather these things together for yourself, as they can really come in handy as you're Staging your house.

Nails and screws in different sizes.
Pens, pencils, and Magic Markers.
Assorted picture hangers, brads, pins, and hooks.
Hammers, staple gun, and screwdriver assortment.
Utility knife, pliers, and wire cutters.
Small cordless drill/screwdriver.
Assorted lightbulbs, extension cords, and timers.
Measuring tape, stud finder, and small level.
Furniture mark fill-in sticks in different colors.
Tissue paper in different colors.
Ribbon, fishing line, rope, string, and twine.

Paper towels, toilet paper, twist ties, and rubber bands.

Window cleaner and furniture cleaner wipes.

Scissors, needle and thread, safety pins.

Electrical tape, Scotch tape, masking tape.

Spackle, glue, and Wite-Out.

Small step stool or ladder.

Furniture-lifting tool and felt-bottom furniture slides.

Handheld steamer.

Mini vacuum.

Dust cloths.

Garbage bags that stand by themselves.

Krud Kutter.

Rubber gloves.

BARGAINS AT THE GROCERY STORE

I love Staging from the grocery store. It is a gold mine of Staging props. I've discovered some of my best Staging bargains in the aisles of my local supermarket when I was buying things for dinner. I've found bouquets of curly willow, elegant bath towels, and suede pillows for $7. I have a grocery-store afghan with tasseled corners ($9.99) that I've draped on a sofa and also used as a rug, under a $65 wicker trunk (which I also found at the grocery store). I love to find bargains like this. The only problem is fitting all my finds into my sweet yellow VW Beetle, Lilie!

I STAGE, THEREFORE I SHOP

When you're gathering props for Staging, consider quality, look, cost, and availability. Why invest $150 in a wicker trunk when you can get one with the same look for $65 and have money left over for other Staging supplies? Here are some of the places (in no particular order) where I've found wonderful things to use in Staging:

Target	Thrift shops
Pier 1	Home Depot
Cost Plus	Michaels
Ikea	Jo-ann Fabrics
Kmart	Garage sales
T.J. Maxx	Costco
Tuesday Morning	Marshalls
Lowe's	Linens N Things
Ross	Bed Bath & Beyond
Wal-Mart	Ace Hardware
Fred Meyer	

There are many more wonderful shops, of course, but those listed here have stores located in most parts of the country. Shop your local boutiques, too, as I do.

If your favorite store is not on my list, that just means I haven't found it yet! Let me know what your favorite store is. I would love to hear from you.

PICNIC-AISLE HEADBOARD

In the picnic aisle of the grocery store, I envisioned the perfect headboard for a child's room when I saw paper plates shaped like animal faces. I bought them, took them to the house I was Staging, and nailed nine plates to the wall above a twin bed: five in the bottom row and three above that, with a single plate at the top. (Again, always use an odd number of things; it's more pleasing to the eye.) Raffia whiskers, bandana neckerchiefs, and glued-on button eyes completed the setup, all for pennies. When the house was sold, the buyers insisted that we leave the headboard for their son. They actually wrote the headboard I had made into the purchase and sale contract! The seller was pleased, too, and thought I walked on water. Staging works!

THE EYES OF A STAGER

Start looking at the world like a Home Stager does. Maybe you already do. Asking "How can I use this in a different way?" is a habit that is almost addictive. When you Stage your home, it will be just the way you want it to be—until you get that next big rush of creativity and start Staging anew! It just gets better and better.

If you are excited by all that you are learning, become an ASP with me and build your own Home Staging business. For more information, contact www.StagedHomes.com.

CHAPTER 7

SHOWING YOUR STAGED HOUSE: LIGHTS! MUSIC! ACTION!

Think about your favorite store: the way it looks, the music that's playing, the way you feel when you step inside. That's the mood you want to re-create when you Stage your house. Appeal to the emotions of the buyer, and the agents, appraisers, and inspectors, too. All these people are crucial to the sale of your house. Once you've Staged your house, keep it Staged every day so it really pays off for you. If you went to your favorite store and the lights were off, you wouldn't go in. If it was dirty and there were clothes all over the floor, you wouldn't want to buy there. The same is true of your house. When it is for sale, you want lights on, music playing, and plenty of space for buyers to move around. This allows them to mentally move into your home so they will want to make it their own.

Personally, I like Target stores. The aisles are wide, the music is right, the light is bright, the merchandise is well stocked, and you can pick up a phone and find someone to help you right away. This is a Staged store! They have their act together, and they are not paying me to tell you this—at this point, they don't know me from Adam (or Eve).

Here are some of my hot Staging tips that will help sell your house for top dollar.

- Turn on all lights and lamps. A home that's bright looks larger. If you're at work, put the lights on timers, especially from 10 in the morning until 6 at night, the usual showing times.

- Open all curtains and blinds, unless the view is miserable. I'm always amazed when I show a house and the curtains are drawn. Some owners say they don't want their furniture to fade, and to them I say, "This is temporary—and you won't have a new house to move into if you don't get this one sold. We're selling your house, not the furniture, so let's leave the curtains open." Buyers only know what they see, not the way it's going to be. Let in the light before the buyers arrive. If your windows open to an unsightly view, put up sheer drapes that let light in and filter the view.

- Keep music playing all the time; you never know when a showing may take place. Choose an easy-listening station and set the volume low. You can put your radios on timers, too. If your house has more than one level, make sure all radios are tuned to the same station. No hard rock or funeral music. Just "elevator music"—gentle and low. You can even put up a little sign that says "Please keep the music on." I can't tell you how many agents will shut off the music (except for ASP real estate agents, who know how to market and sell a house!).

- Make sure all toilet lids are down. I have to admit, this is one of my pet peeves. You're not selling the holes in your house, but that's what it looks like when you keep the toilet lid up.

- Hide the wastebaskets. I really don't like seeing wastebaskets. After all, they have garbage in them. Whether you are selling or not, put them somewhere out of sight—under the sink or in a cupboard, in a closet or a pantry. Clean them, too, and empty the wastebaskets every day. I feel good when I empty the garbage because I am actually getting rid of the garbage in and around my life. You will, too. Your house will look better, whether you're selling a Staged house or living in one. "Less garbage, less stress," I always say. Think about it: Buyers pick up on so many small, subtle details, and sometimes they aren't even aware of why they like or dislike a property. If they see garbage, they may get a subconscious feeling that the house isn't well taken care of. If so, they'll move on and never know the potential of your house. Don't let that happen to you over something as simple as emptying the garbage.

- Close the garage doors. Most garages don't look that great on the inside. Paint the door inside or out if it is badly marked. Make sure the track is working so the door moves smoothly up and down.

- Inside the garage, sweep the floor and clean it with a degreaser. If you have a workbench, clean that off, too. In the lower end of the market, it's fine to pack things neatly in one corner of the garage. But if your house is listed at the top end of the market, empty the garage as best you can, and paint the floor with gray cement paint so it looks like you could eat off it! The more costly your home, the less you should see in the garage.

- Empty the carport. It should have nothing in it except the car. When buyers drive up to a house with a carport, they see everything, so there should be nothing to see. A carport looks bigger when it's empty, too. If there are garbage cans, children's toys, or a woodpile in your carport, move them to a less obvious place or throw them out. What people see is either a turn-on or a turnoff. We're working on making you money, so even the smallest things matter.

- Give potential buyers privacy as they view your home. It's best to leave the house when an agent stops by for a showing. Buyers need space to fall in love with your house, and to talk about it without you listening in. You can take a walk or work in the yard or garden, in which case you're nearby to answer any questions that might come up during the showing. Let them come to you; do not go to them. I promise you that when they love your house they will want to ask you questions, and I know you will be happy to answer!

- After someone comes to see your house, the showing agent should leave a business card. Each night, call your listing agent with the showing agent's name, company, phone numbers, and e-mail address, so your listing agent can follow up. (I always recommend listing your house with an ASP real estate agent. Go to www.StagedHomes.com to find an ASP real estate agent in your area. Call at least three, interview them, and decide on the one that's right for you. They are specially trained to serve you in the best way possible.)

> **TIP**
>
> SELLER: I've got kids! How can I Stage?
>
> BARB: Make Staging a game. Ask three- to five-year-olds to make a pile of their very favorite things. Feature the things they select in a wagon, a fun toy box, or a doll carriage, as part of your Staging. All other toys can be packed away for the new house. Together with your kids, write on that box, "TOYS: OPEN FIRST IN NEW HOUSE." Once you move, your kids will be so happy to see their toys that you will have (a bit of) time to unpack, as you begin to Stage to Live in your new home.

Give older children a Staging reward. If the reward is money, give them half when they Stage their rooms and the rest when the house sells and closes. Or set a goal the whole family can enjoy after the house sells (a trip to Disneyland, a camping weekend, or something like that) and tell the kids, "Every day you Stage takes us closer to Disneyland." Take it from me, this really works.

LIVING THROUGH THE SELLING PROCESS IN A STAGED HOME

It's hard to keep a house in tip-top shape through the selling process, especially when there's a baby, pets, or children in the house.

But believe me, it's temporary, and it won't be long until your house is sold and you're on your way to new places. Give everyone in the family a Staging job to do each day so everyone has a role and you don't have to do it all yourself. When everyone pitches in, Staging is more fun than ever.

If you have pets, as I do, decide what you'll do with them when your house is being shown. A shady outdoor kennel, a pet walker, doggie day care? Decide on a plan that's ready to be put into action as needed. If you have indoor cats, confine them to one room where their needs are met and put a sign on the door so they don't get out. Some people are afraid of reptiles; you may have to Stage that pet snake or iguana right over to a neighbor's house while yours is being sold. Don't worry; they'll be back soon. As I said, it's temporary.

CHAPTER 8

WELCOME TO BARB'S HOUSE: STAGING TO LIVE!

Staging to Live means having less stuff in your life. Stuff brings stress. The more you have, the more you have to take care of, and that means less time for you. More stuff, more stress. This vicious cycle goes on and on, until you put a stop to it. Yes, our homes feature belongings that we love and enjoy. That's great, but how can we see them all when so many other things are in the way? The impact of clutter is very strong. It can make children crabby and adults bicker. In a cluttered home, people's attention is pulled in so many directions it doesn't know where to focus. You simply cannot look at everything.

Staging to Live helps you work through the clutter step by step. Staging to Live clears space in your house so everyone who lives there can find more peace and joy. Our research shows that Staging to Sell helps buyers see a home more easily, and Staging to Live helps you see your own home more clearly. When you balance your life with fewer things, you'll feel freer in your own home. I am on a mission to focus on space and life. Staging can become a way of life.

People often ask me, "Barb, what is your house like? Is your house Staged?" Well, I must tell you (no surprise), my house is Staged. I don't go to work without Staging the house. Before I go to bed, I Stage the house. When my cousin came to visit years ago, she noticed that I don't leave the house without Staging it for my return. And she saw a whole new way of living. Instead of coming home to toothpaste and towels left out, you can destress the environment you live in and come home to peace, quiet, and a feeling of joy.

I like walking into a Staged environment; I feel out of alignment if a room isn't Staged. It must be something in my genes. Everything has a place, and if it doesn't, I can sell it, give it to someone I care about, give it to someone I don't even know, or use it to Stage my next client's home. Every time I bring something new into my house, something else must go: That's my rule. I love things—yes, I do—but I love people and space even more. Get rid of it if you don't need it.

That said, I also believe in living with the things you love. Why wait until company comes to use your best dishes and quilts, to have fresh flowers, to burn candles? If you wait for guests, you may never have a chance to really enjoy the things you love. What is the worst thing that can happen to them? Not a lot. If something is too special to live with, pack it up and put it away. Otherwise, have your favorite things around you always. Wear the things you love, and wear them now. Get them out of your closet. There is no better time than the present, and that is all we ever have anyway. I agree with that aphorism that says "Today is a gift and that is why it is called the present." Cool, huh?

STAGING TO LIVE

When you're Staging to Live, here are a few questions to ask yourself weekly, or even daily: Is there anything in this room that can be removed now or moved to another place in the house? What can I live without? In the kitchen, what can you put away? Should the coffee grinder go? Can I do without the electric knife? A bit of vigilance can keep appliances from taking over your kitchen. Do the same inventory in every room. Moving just one thing can change everything, and everything is interdependent. When you're selling a house, let the house shine. When you live in a house, you need space for *you*. Staging to Live just plain feels good.

STAGING TO LIVE AT MY HOUSE

Welcome to my home! A planter outside my front door is lined with moss and filled with impatiens in various shades of pink and white, with an ivy topiary in the center.

There are stargazer lilies in the front hall that make the whole house smell delightful. Can you smell them? I bet you can! They are so beautiful. I love lilies.

Everything is clean, fresh, and polished, just the way I like it. (If you need help cleaning, hire someone. You can also trade services with a friend—for example, babysitting in exchange for housecleaning, or any trade that makes sense. This works, and can be a win-win for both parties.)

My furniture is large and spare and comfortable. I like to

A STAGING-TO-LIVE STORY

One day a woman decides to redecorate her house. She gets a bid, which comes in at $3,500. When her husband comes home, she shares her exciting news with him and he hits the roof! "Thirty-five-hundred dollars to redecorate? You have to be kidding me!" he exclaims. He has no incentive for doing this. She is motivated, but he is not. He tells her that his chair has been in that spot in that room for more than 15 years and he isn't going to allow that chair to be moved anywhere. So she doesn't redecorate.

Three months later he comes home with news of his own. "Honey," he says, "you aren't going to believe this, but we are being transferred to Dallas, and they are doubling my pay. It's only for three years, and we will make so much more money. We'll save on living expenses compared to our city, and after three years we can come back here." He continues, "On the plane the other day when I was flying back from my business trip, I read in the Southwest Airlines magazine about Home Staging and this woman, Barb Schwarz, who came up with the concept. It sounds like we can sell our home for even more by Staging it! So we should get on the Internet right now and find the right ASP to help us do that!"

The couple calls an ASP, who comes out to the house, takes pictures, makes detailed notes, and comes back with a plan and a bid of $3,500 for Home Staging. The husband says, "We have to do this. It will help us get more money for the house!"

Do you recognize the difference in motivation here? The husband saw no reason to redecorate; he didn't have any incentive to do so. But he recognized the wisdom of Staging. Without the proper motivation, nothing happens. Decorating is optional, but Staging is mandatory.

What happens next? The couple leave the house while it is being Staged and come back that night. He says, "This is incredible! We should have

Continued

done this when we lived here. The house feels so much bigger. I feel freer in my own home." He asks the Stager, "We're selling this house, but after we move, can you come and help us Stage our new place in Dallas?" Once again, he has the motivation. People will progress from Staging to Sell to Staging to Live—it's only natural. A Staged home looks and feels more relaxing. Staging usually costs less than redecorating. And there is more space to enjoy with your family. Home Staging to Sell (HSTS) and Home Staging to Live (HSTL) make sense. I predict a day when most people will Stage to Live because it feels so much better than living in a house that is not Staged. Staging is my joy and passion, and I'm delighted to share my creation with you.

put large pieces in smaller rooms, because it makes the rooms look larger. There is a point of no return with this, though; when a room starts to feel crowded, stop! In making decisions, I let my creativity rule. The only time I seem to make mistakes is when I don't lead my life that way.

Plush light beige wall-to-wall carpeting flows throughout the house, spilling into every room as water would, creating a gentle, neutral background.

There are a lot of animal prints around: zebra, leopard, cheetah, and ocelot. I love the look; however, it's easy to overdo animal prints. Buy just enough to give you the feeling without letting the jungle take over.

I don't have much need for curtains at my house, so there are white California shutters on the windows instead.

When you need an afghan, there it is, draped over the side

of the ottoman, chair, piano, or table. I have many of these; you can never have too many. I get them on sale at T.J. Maxx. They're lovely and don't cost much—about $16 each. I also keep them out on the patio, as it gets a bit chilly at night. If it rains on them, so what?

You smile, because there's a butterfly pillow on the chair and painted rocks on the table that say "Wild Woman."

A friendly green frog sits on top of the tall standing clock in my family room, watching the time go by. I let him keep track, because I don't believe in time. I always say, "We have all the time we need to get things done," and it always turns out to be true. I believe we are spiritual beings on a human journey. But I digress . . .

On my family room mantel, rather than something serious, you will find exploding bouquets of party spangles on wire stems, bursting from huge red goblets.

Things are organized. This makes it easier to accomplish everything I need to do. There is a place for everything, and everything's in its place.

There is healthy food in the pantry and dog bones in the cupboard. I'm a good cook, but these days I don't cook like I used to. I keep snacks in the refrigerator, and we order takeout a lot. When I have friends over, I cook some of the dinner and pick up the rest on my way home, so it's ready to serve. Time with my friends is more important to me now than slaving over a hot stove.

There is a plentiful supply of water in the pantry. I drink a lot of water. We can live without food for quite some time, but not without water.

I eat lightly. I've found that it's so much better for me to eat small meals three to five times a day. As I get "younger," I just don't need as much food as I used to. Eating lighter and eating smaller portions works for me now.

You are probably like me: I like my kitchen sink to be immaculate. My dishwashing soap pumps from a china soap dispenser, with a pretty, jeweled votive candle cup alongside. That's it! The sponge rests against the back of the sink in its own stick-on holder from the kitchen shop or Bed Bath & Beyond. These fantastic little inventions stick to the inside of the sink, so the sponge doesn't have to sit on the top of the sink. I keep everything else under the sink, organized in low plastic dishpans.

The lamp on my kitchen counter is a straw wine jug lying on its side, wrapped with tendrils of ivy. It's stuffed with white Christmas lights and glows softly. I leave it on all the time, since the voltage is so low. The effect is lovely, day or night.

I keep napkins in the same drawer as the silverware, so when you grab a spoon, you grab a napkin. The silverware drawer is lined with a zebra-print cloth napkin that always makes me smile.

I love packs of pretty cocktail napkins. I keep them stacked in the kitchen cupboards, ready to go. You never know when a party will start!

My baby grand piano is beautiful, but I haven't played her for a while. I just decided to move her to my office in another city. She looks great there, and when we have an office function, she can be played and enjoyed.

I don't have any ditsy little things around; I don't need them anymore.

The beds are piled with pretty pillows edged with beads,

sparkles, and fancy trim. When my brother-in-law comes to visit, I use more masculine pillows in the guest room. It's fun to change them all the time and move the pillows from room to room.

I love tassels, don't you? I hang tassels from my doorknobs and the cupboard doors, on lamps and teddy bears for accents, and on towels that are for display only. They are in almost every room in my home. Shop around to find the best ones at the best price.

Plenty of new hangers fill the closets. There are no wire hangers anywhere; I recycle those back to the dry cleaner. All my hangers are either white plastic or the padded ones I buy at Tuesday Morning, where they often have them on sale at good prices.

In my walk-in guest room closet there's a small table, lamp, mirror, and Kleenex on a tray, with a brush and toiletries for my guests. They can use them and take them home when they leave. I love Staging for my guests. I want them to feel at home and experience the spaciousness that Staging always provides.

I hang lots of big mirrors everywhere, in beautiful frames, so every room feels expansive and full of light. The look can be expensive, but I've found great buys at my favorite stores. Mirrors make any room seem bigger, especially a bathroom.

Silk orchids, white lilies, and elephant leaves fill in for real plants sometimes. I love the look of silk orchids in the bathrooms, and they look so real.

The bathroom rugs aren't bathroom rugs. They are big, pretty leopard-patterned throw rugs (not real, of course), or ones with an Asian look. I don't like fuzzy bathroom rugs. They trap dirt and give me the fuzz creeps. My rugs come from Target, Wal-Mart, and some of my other favorite stores.

It was your home; now it's a house—a product you're selling. When you Stage, make it look better than any other house on the market. Make the bed, bring in a small table vignette as we did here, and your bedroom is Staged! Open the blinds to sell the view; you can't sell it if you can't see it.

Painting the walls and adding a strong piece of artwork can give a bathroom fresh appeal. This painting used to be hidden near the refrigerator in the kitchen; we moved it to make better use of it.

Staging can transform any family room from cluttered to charming. We put away all the little things and brought in a plant, a standing lamp from another room, and an armoire that was taking up too much space in one of the bedrooms. Can you tell that the rug under the trunk is actually an inexpensive afghan?

You can't sell it if you can't see it. Cutting and trimming the bushes revealed a gorgeous home with a fountain in front that really shows well now. Always trim trees from the bottom up and bushes from the top down. Now this home is Staged!

Clutter eats your equity. Simply clearing the countertops and packing away personal items Staged this kitchen. Overhead is a very special chandelier, and now a buyer can really see and appreciate the room.

Put some things away; shift the furniture; turn on all the lights: This gives the room a new flavor. A plant was brought in, and a painting moved upstairs from the basement. The Staged room is lighter and softer, like a face with less eyeliner.

To Stage this large, empty house, the buyer simply needed to see where the furniture could go, and revel in the fabulous space. I rented furniture and brought in some carefully edited items for the shelves. Staging vacant properties is crucial to allow the buyer to mentally move in before buying.

This house was partly furnished, but many rooms were empty. The Staging budget was modest; creativity solved that problem. The dining table is a plastic one from Lowe's, covered with a sheet and a tapestry table topper. The wicker chairs were on sale at Pier 1. I added the ficus tree and a centerpiece, and set the table. The house sold in record time for top dollar. Staging works!

Decluttering is so important. Clearing off the countertop helped sell this Staged kitchen.

In a child's room, a good rule of thumb is to remove at least 50 percent of the contents to Stage it for sale. Moving the bed and adding snowy white gauze at the window added a sweet touch. I found the gauze in the seller's linen closet.

Changing the traffic flow gave this Staged room a much larger look. Before, the room looked sad and worn. Now that it is Staged, it says, "Come in and buy me!" What a difference Staging makes!

When you're Staging, don't overdo; that's the opposite of what Staging is all about! Take away a few chairs, add a no-cost arrangement of branches from outdoors, and—Bingo!—this condominium kitchen has a theme. Putting the table against the wall is an easy way to make the space seem so much larger.

You Stage so that buyers can mentally move in, and that won't happen if a room isn't inviting. This guest room had no personality, but once it was Staged it became so inviting that buyers could imagine buying the house and welcoming friends to this room. This is one of the rooms we Staged for ABC's *20/20* show.

Depersonalizing a room allows buyers to mentally move in. See how sophisticated the Staged look is? The boring, scattered look has been replaced by a classier decor and a much more spacious feeling. The leather furniture was crowding the living room, but works just perfectly here.

Removing the heavy, freestanding wall units gave this dining room the bright, open look buyers love. This home sold in record time.

A lacy tablecloth and an ivy clipping become a creative no-cost window treatment.

Fresh tricks: In a Staged bathroom, tying up the towels makes them look their best (and keeps buyers from wiping their hands on them!). Stick a blossom in the ribbon for an easy accent.

I have a straw ostrich named Lucy, who lives in the shower and wears special outfits for all the holidays. Guests always laugh when they see Lucy in the shower during one of my parties or dinner gatherings. She's about five feet tall, she's very attractive, and she's very "hip."

There are no wastebaskets in view—none! They hide behind the toilet or in the cabinet under each sink.

I have a cat named Annie, and Sophie, the big yellow lab. Sophie's water dish is a huge white bowl with a flower on the bottom; Isaac Mizrahi designed it for Target. Nothing but the best for my fur child!

I have also Staged my garage. Well, gee, why not? I have placed a leopard runner in the garage between my two cars. The garage floor is freshly painted. I keep my garage tidy. I enjoy driving into the garage more that way after traveling or a long day at the office.

I drive a yellow VW Beetle named Lilie. There are show tunes on the CD player and a bouquet of flowers in the vase on the dashboard. Those VW people really know how to Stage a car to sell it! It's my first VW, and I love it.

Outside, there are several seating areas on my patio, not just one. Six oversized chairs circle a round coffee table, anchored by a big rectangular sisal rug edged in burgundy. I consider the outdoors to be a room; why not Stage it? Decks, patios, and balconies can get the same treatment. Let your creativity soar!

You're soothed by the peaceful sound of water trickling from my hot tub to the pool in the backyard. If you don't have a pool, you can install a small or large fountain out back or by the front door so the sound of moving water is always close by. I love the sound of water, don't you? It's so calming and relaxing.

A rubber duckie wearing black sunglasses floats in the pool, and her baby floats in the hot tub (she also wears sunglasses—it's sunny out here in California!).

Then there's Uncle Henry. He's electronic and lives in the pool eating nature—in the form of bugs, leaves, and dirt. He does a great job of cleaning (I mean Staging) the pool. Thank you, Uncle Henry!

Because I am a night person, I stay up later than some. That's when you'll find me Staging my home. I make changes each week in at least one room. Moving things around keeps me aware of what's around me, so that I really see things as they are. Think about it: When things settle into a routine or pattern, you stop seeing them. Make a change—hang a picture, move a chair—and all of a sudden you see the room anew.

Well, I don't have room to share everything about my home, but I've given you a glimpse, and hopefully a few ideas as well. I love living in a Staged home, and I think you will, too. Whether you're Staging to Live or Staging to Sell, a Staged home has magic—the magic you bring to it. Remember, you are the director, the actor, the producer, and the set designer of your life, so have fun, live life to the fullest, and make your space a Staged one! I know you will love what Staging can do in so many areas of your life. It's a new way of living. Happy Staging and Happy Living!

CHAPTER 9

WHAT DO YOU DO WHEN YOU NEED HELP? ASPs TO THE RESCUE!

Home Staging is so important and can really help sell your property. However, you might be saying, "I love the idea of Staging my home for sale, but I'm just not a 'vision person.'" Or, "I'm having trouble seeing my house with an unemotional eye." If you'd like someone else to help Stage your home, you can hire an Accredited Staging Professional (ASP). When you do, you can be sure your home is in good hands.

ASPs are taught to prepare your home according to the Home Staging principles and practices that I have developed. ASPs are trained to see the positives in your property, and they can help you set the Stage, so you can sell the space in your home for the highest price possible in the least amount of time. This is true for any market, and for any market condition. ASPs have successfully completed a detailed ASP course and passed a thorough examination on preparing homes for sale. They have graduated from the StagedHomes.com course in Home Staging and are ready to use their unique skills to Stage your home professionally, both inside and out.

It's easy to find an ASP in your area by logging on to www.StagedHomes.com (1-800-392-7161) and entering your zip code and city. ASPs are always willing to share references, and the web site shows homes they've recently Staged. After your home has been Staged, your ASP can place it in the For Sale part of our StagedHomes.com web site, where your property can be seen by millions of potential buyers. Only Staged homes are listed on our site. This is a wonderful way for buyers to learn about Staged homes for sale. It really does help them find the right home for themselves, which might be, and could be, your house! On the site, you can also purchase products and supplies that I recommend to help you Stage your home.

You can hire an ASP (or an ASPM—an Accredited Staging Professional Master—who has additional training) to perform two kinds of services for you: a Home Staging consultation or a bid.

A Home Staging consultation is a written plan, usually 20 pages or more, with ideas and a description of what needs to be done to Stage your house, room by room, inside and out. You do the actual work yourself, enacting each suggestion. Your investment for the consultation usually falls in the $300 to $500 range, but it varies according to the size of your house, how much clutter there is in your house, and the region of the country in which you live. An experienced ASP who has Staged thousands of houses may charge a higher fee than an ASP who is just starting out. I encourage you to e-mail or call several ASPs. Your intuition will tell you when you've found the ASP who can best meet your needs. Some ASPs even do Home Staging consultations online, by exchanging pictures and e-mails with you.

An ASP or ASPM can also prepare a bid to let you know what the fee and services would be if they Stage your house for you. There is no charge for a bid. It lists the rooms to be Staged and the services that will be provided as part of the Staging process. There is no obligation when you ask for a bid. Once a bid has been prepared and presented, owners generally do hire the ASP or ASPM to perform the services outlined, because it is much more convenient and efficient than doing the work themselves. Time is money, and with people's obligations coming from so many different directions, it just makes sense to hire an accredited professional to Stage your house. This allows you to get on with your life while your house is being Staged and sold for top dollar. Again, the service fee will vary according to the size of your home, the amount of clutter, the area of the country in which you live, and the amount of work to be performed. Normally, the fee to have your home Staged ranges from $1,000 to $3,500 or more. You might think this figure high, but if you compare it to the amount of equity you have in your house and what you hope to obtain when it sells, this is a sensible investment—especially when your house sells quicker and for more money than you ever thought possible. Like the commission you pay to a real estate agent, the Staging fee brings results. It is an investment in achieving your goal—a closed sale on your property—and it's an investment that really works!

I recently had a client whose cluttered house had been sitting on the market in poor condition for more than 10 months.

He never got an offer. He spent $17,000 improving the condition of his home, including painting and weeding, and $8,000 to Stage, which made it look like an entirely different property. The house sold for $1.9 million. That's an 8,000 percent return on his money. It is hard to get that kind of return on any investment these days!

DO YOU WANT TO BECOME AN ASP?

As the creator of the Home Staging industry, I developed the ASP designation because I believed that professional status and credentials were essential. I have worked to build this industry for more than 33 years. I believe in the entrepreneurial spirit. And though some people have a knack for decorating, Home Staging is not decorating, nor is it design. It is a way to sell homes. It's crucial to understand how the real estate industry works, what buyers are looking for, and how they behave. Furthermore, the degree of creativity that an ASP brings to the process of selling a home is so much greater than that of someone who simply purchases some furniture and drapes, the way some so-called Stagers do.

I offer ASP training all over the United States and Canada, and even in some other countries as well. You can go to our web site, www.StagedHomes.com, to request information about becoming an ASP. Or call our office at 1-800-392-7161. We will be happy to answer your questions. Becoming an ASP and doing creative work in the service of others makes the world a better place. And that's what our ASPs are all about.

A FEW LAST WORDS TO YOU

I believe in you. I believe in the talent and wonderful creativity we all have as human beings. When you allow that talent and creativity to work through you for the greater good of all concerned, you are a gift to many people. Think about everyone you serve through your family connections, your work, your church, and your school—the list goes on and on.

I also know we are all interdependent on one another. The world is a Stage, and no matter what is happening in your life, you can Stage it. I bought a card the other day that said: "Do the best you can with what you have been given in the time you have." I thought of Home Staging when I saw that card. Home Staging is not about buying a lot of unnecessary furniture or accessories. If you already have many possessions, then, by all means, use them. And if you do need more things, buy them. But be selective and compare as you buy. Paint can perform miracles; wallpaper often doesn't—it's too much a matter of personal taste and preference. Yes, move things in and take things out; most homes have too much in them. Greenery can heal a room. And always keep in mind that less is more. Nevertheless, your creativity is the most important factor. Creativity uses all you have to achieve the look with the most impact. Acknowledge that you can Stage your home and make it work for you. I have seen thousands of Staged homes sell quicker and for more money, and I know this can happen for you, too.

CHAPTER 10

STAGING TALES FROM THE TRENCHES

Staging is setting the scene so it appeals to most people. A well-Staged home allows potential buyers to experience the house (the *product*). Here are some true-life Staging stories that prove how powerful Staging can be. I'm sure that many of these situations will strike a familiar chord with you.

SIMPLE STAGING GETS RESULTS

A prospective client saw my web site and gave me a call. She had had her house on the market for more than 90 days with no offers and very few showings. It was in a good neighborhood, had a nice floor plan, was well priced, and really should have sold. I met her at the house to discuss Staging. The minute I walked in I realized one of the main problems: The house was dark. It was a vacant home and, thinking of security, the seller was keeping all the blinds closed. I talked to her about the need for the house to be light and bright. There were a couple of other minor issues, too. She asked me to Stage it.

The next day, a Friday, I Staged the home, which involved mostly accessorizing and arranging a couple of sitting areas—one in the living room and another in the master bedroom. We opened all the window blinds and drew back the curtains covering other windows. Her real estate agent held an open house over the weekend. Monday morning she called to tell me that she and her husband had received two offers, both more than the asking price.

This is what Staging is all about. As a real estate agent and a Stager, I have a great network with other agents. As our local market is changing, listing inventory is up, houses are taking longer to sell, and more price reduction is going on. I can't wait to see the increase in Staging business!

Mary Helen Ivers, ASP
Staging Solutions
Roseville, California

BUYERS LINE UP TO SEE THE TRANSFORMATION

This tired house had been purchased months ago by an investment seller. The original plan had been to "flip" the home, but that idea had fallen by the wayside. Now the house needed to be marketed and merchandised to sell. Sadly, the home had some cosmetic maintenance issues: flesh-colored paint throughout and carpet that had turned from white to gray. The original owners had sold in three days due to economic circumstances, and the house reflected the stress of its former inhabitants. The seller didn't have a listing agent yet, so I immediately recommended the ASP real estate agent I work with, who understands and values the benefits of Staging. Together, we met the investment seller, toured the home, and showed our marketing plans and Career Books (our personal portfolios). The seller listed the home with the ASP real estate agent that afternoon.

We spent a month repainting, recarpeting, cleaning grout, dealing with maintenance issues, and installing new tile in the master bath. We set the Stage to sell. We installed furniture and decor with help from some new ASP apprentices in our area, and buyers were chomping at the bit to get inside. The house was shown on demand, with two cabinets yet to be installed, but all the Staging was in place by then. The house went into contract within a week, at $100,000 over the appraised value! The newly merchandised house was showcased with color, a good cleaning, and a lot of love. The gleaming granite counters now popped with color, the windows and sliders showed off the pool and waterfront, and the house boasted clean tile and new carpeting. The Staged furnishings defined each room, created a large, open sense of space, and filled the home with positive joy.

Kelly McFrederick, ASPM, IAHSP
Kelly's Staging Kreations
Belle Air, Florida

LIGHTING IT UP IN FLORIDA

One of the most beautiful condominiums on the island of Tierra Verde, Florida, sat vacant and for sale for 400 days. It had dismal curb appeal. As you stepped off the elevator at the condo's private entrance, the foyer light had been permanently extinguished, creating an immediate feeling of gloom. Inside, the granite counters were dusty and the toilets sat open, showing off unhealthy and dirty hard-water deposits. Bird droppings were spattered on the terrace mats, and the side shutters were thrown open to show an ugly pink condo next door. The sellers were frustrated as their mortgage payments continued month after month with no buyers in sight for this slightly dusty jewel overlooking the Grand Canal, where speedboats paraded their sporty colors.

We started Staging the week before Christmas, with the goal of highlighting interior features as well as the breathtaking views. First on the list: a detailed cleaning, new light fixtures, and new lightbulbs to replace all those that had simply burned out and had never been replaced. Even these small steps made a huge difference. Shutters were adjusted to reflect the light and beauty within, and we also set an emotional stage so buyers could mentally move in. This condo was featured in a tour of Staged properties for sale, and all the condo association's neighbors and all interested buyers and potential sellers were invited to take a look. Within 18 days this now-beautiful condo sold for full value, after more than a year on the market. What a Christmas gift for the sellers!

Kelly McFrederick, ASPM, IAHSP
Kelly's Staging Kreations
Belle Air, Florida

FROM WHITE TO WARM IN DALLAS

For four months in 2004, this gorgeous home in one of the most desirable neighborhoods of Dallas sat on the market, so the owner gave up and pulled it off the market. Eight months later, I received a call from Scott, the home-owner, asking me to come over and do a Staging consultation on his home. When I arrived and knocked on the front door, I was greeted by the most wonderful family—Scott, and his wife, Janis, and their four beautiful little girls. As I entered the home, my first impression was how cold the house felt. There were white floors, white cabinets, white countertops, and outdated wallpaper. There was very little color in the house except in the girls' rooms, which were precious. After my tour of the house, I went back to my office and wrote up my "Scope of Work" report for the entire house. The next day, I met with Scott to go over all that needed to be done. Together we came up with a game plan for who would be responsible for each item on the list. It took two months for Scott and Janis to replace the carpet, strip the wallpaper and repaint the guest bathroom and massive kitchen, and complete all the needed repair work.

Then I came back to do my "Staging magic." I brought in some slip-covers, plants, and accessories. In a couple of days, the house was totally transformed, popping with color and life! Scott, Janis, and the girls were thrilled at the transformation. Scott called the real estate agent to list his home, and three weeks later, they received a full-price offer! I love to see successes like this one, and I appreciate the fact that, in this family's eyes, I've helped change their lives for the better. Although they now live in another state, we still keep in touch via e-mail.

As a side note, I was Staging the living room one day when Scott left a large box in the foyer. Two of the little girls began playing in the box, and I overheard them say, "Let's Stage the box." So they did, bringing in pillows and a plant. Could this be our next generation of Stagers? I think so!

Bette Vos, ASP, IAHSP
Showtime! Staging and Organizing
Rowlett, Texas

STAGED, IT SOLD IN 30 MINUTES!

Shortly after receiving my ASP designation, my husband and I decided to relocate from California to Idaho, so I Staged our house to sell. We lived on La Contenta golf course, and our large windows were bare so we could enjoy the beautiful views from front and back. This was great for living, but the windows weren't decorated the way they needed to be to sell the house and the view. As Barb says, "Buyers only know what they see, not the way it's going to be." So I purchased some foam forms, bought golf-theme material, and began the project of making cornices. The lady at the home show made it look so easy. After much laughter and messed-up material, my husband, Jim, and I finally got it right. We were so impressed we ended up making cornices for the entire room, including the 10-foot window. We already had a conversation area in the living room. Now when you entered the door, the cornices framed a beautiful backdrop—the golf course, pond, and willows. It really had the "Wow Factor" that Barb talks about, and we had invested less than $200.

I rearranged the dining room table, took out the two leaves, removed some chairs, and added a picture, and the room looked softer.

I had a collection of chef dolls and apples in the kitchen, which hid the beauty of my black Silestone counter and white custom cabinets. Several items were packed up (after all, I was moving wasn't I?). The kitchen sparkled like never before.

As a real estate agent and Stager, my professional documents were always in order, but my personal papers were another matter. That part of the office looked like a fumble on the 40-yard line. I finally Staged my bookcase, filed household papers, opened the double doors, and—va-voom!—the room was welcoming.

By this time, Jim thought I had flipped, so like a good Stager, I reminded him that "the way we live in our home and the way we market and sell the house are two different things."

The guest room was next, and it was fully loaded with toys for the grandchildren. The shelves seemed to burst with family pictures and "stuff."

(continued)

We packed the keepsakes, sent the toys to the grandkids, and donated the rest to charity. I arranged the wrought-iron trundle bed at an angle, draped it with a wine-colored throw, and added toss pillows and a huge Pooh bear. I pulled two guitars out of their cases and Staged them in the corner. Wow, what a transformation!

The master closet was 10 feet by 5 feet, with the clothes hung according to color. Jim kept clothes in several sizes, and he was not a happy seller when I asked him to discard the things he couldn't wear. As with my clients, I had to "inform before I performed." He ever so reluctantly sorted out the things that fit and gave the rest away. We keep our shoes organized on shelves; mine were in clear plastic shoeboxes with pictures of each pair taped on the front of the boxes, but Jim wouldn't let me do his that way.

As I reinspected each Staged room, I went "back to the door" for a look. Then it was time for the outside. I found wonderful bright flowers in large hanging pots on sale. For $150 I purchased several pots, which I hung from the arbor along the front porch. This solution looked vibrant and, best of all, was inexpensive. Our porch was a vignette of park-style benches, a glass side table, lawn chairs, and flowers. However, the hedges had suffered over-growth. As the saying goes, "Plants are like children: They grow up," so all the hedges were neatly trimmed. My Staged front porch was an invitation to anyone who drove by or walked up to the house.

The backyard was reminiscent of a Roman coliseum, with two covered patios and cream-colored columns running from the master bedroom to the kitchen along the exterior of the house. Staging the table and lounging area brought added value to the scene.

By 5 P.M. the house was completely Staged, inside and out. As an ASP real estate agent, I installed the company For Sale signs, filled the flyer box, and left for dinner. I received several phone calls about the house, and it wasn't even on the MLS (multiple listing service) yet.

The next morning, Jim and I put out the signs, balloons, and arrows leading the way to the house. Buyers were waiting in the driveway as we arrived home. Within minutes, the place was crawling with prospects, saying, "Wow, this is spectacular." At one point I counted 50 buyers milling around.

(continued)

Several said they were coming back with an offer, but Jim was so over-whelmed that when a buyer gave me a contract with a full-price offer, we accepted it. This was a record. Our Staged home sold in 30 minutes at full price, which was $100,000 over the going market price in the area. Staging works!

Patti B. Walker, ASP, IAHSP
I Stage Homes
Meridian, Idaho

A MILLION-DOLLAR MAKEOVER

I interviewed with a homeowner to give him a bid for Staging. He told me that an interior designer had given him a bid of $125,000. I explained that my goal was to use what he had and accent it with accessories that he could rent. He asked whether I thought I could do it for under $50,000. I laughed! I am charging him only $1,500 per day and $25 per assistant. I am estimating that it will take me two full days. Quite a price difference, no?

Kate Hart, ASP, IAHSP
Katherine Hart Interiors
Philadelphia, Pennsylvania

THE JUDGE SAID, "STAGE"

My first concern was the tone in the real estate agent's voice. I could hear her uneasy hesitation: Could a Stager give her the help she was looking for, or would this be the final stroke in not getting this listing?

Both the sellers, it seemed, were attorneys, and the game was on. Both were sharpening their legal skills in their new life status: divorce.

At the moment, the husband was in residence at this property, but there had been a jockeying for position here. Therein lay the problem. The real estate agent put it this way: "I need you to come and look, because there are some decorating obstacles. Oh, and by the way, the husband called to interview me and I really want this high-end listing, but the wife has her own choice for a real estate agent and she seems to be winning so far. I just thought you should know."

We set a time to meet. The real estate agent sent me out alone. When I arrived, the husband couldn't wait to tell me the gory details, the first of which was instantly obvious to me: All the beautiful furnishings had things missing—the legs had been removed from the dining room table, the kitchen table had only three chairs, and the fourth chair, it seemed, had disappeared. The bookcases were missing their shelves, and a bed from an upstairs bedroom was living in the middle of the library off the foyer. (Apparently, the banishment from the master bedroom had begun here.) Oddities appeared throughout our house tour. For example, there were only washcloths in the baths; the towels had apparently gone to live with the legs from the dining room table.

By the time the real estate agent appeared, Mr. Attorney and I had bonded, and I assured him I could plug in the missing puzzle pieces. He was mysterious about timing, but one thing he was sure of was that he wanted a proposal, in writing. And what about me—what was my role? Would the proposal be prepared on my letterhead? And could I provide references? I spun around, picked up my Career Book (my personal portfolio of my work) and plopped it into his hands. I think that to him, it was as comforting as a legal brief.

(continued)

The real estate agent called me later, saying that she felt she had a competitive chance now and that she was feeling better because the written proposal was on its way. However, there were apparently some legal issues to contend with.

The truth of the matter was that the judge for the divorce proceedings had, of course, been informed about the "battle royal" and the missing furnishings. Mr. Attorney had approached the judge and pleaded that he felt this was intentional sabotage of the sale of the residence. The result: The judge ordered that the house be Staged, as a means of ensuring that the property would sell for a fair market value and in a reasonable amount of time. This sent both parties scurrying. Mrs. Attorney's real estate agent did not use Staging, and wasn't about to start. But Mr. Attorney called my real estate agent and said, "Do you Stage?" I can imagine that her thoughts raced back to my office presentation a couple of months prior to this. She was quick on her feet, and responded, "Of course I do."

The rest is history. We had to wait at least three weeks for the final order to start Staging (enough time to locate the table legs, by the way), and we had an above-asking-price offer right away—the first day, actually!

So that's the verdict: Staging works!

Linda Jenkins, ASPM, IAHSP
Staging Places
Benicia, California

NOW WE CAN RETIRE!

I was called in on a referral from a local real estate agent and friend to Stage a magnificent home in the beautiful city of Grosse Pointe, Michigan. The owners were anxiously waiting to move into a well-deserved retirement home up north, and their $1.6 million mansion had sadly lingered on the market for seven months. Using only their own treasures, which we found in various rooms, the open-minded sellers and I transformed this historic home by Staging. We depersonalized and decluttered, so potential buyers could envision living there. Happily, the first couple who saw this house after it was Staged made an offer and the house was sold! This allowed the sellers to move on to their retirement home. Thank goodness for Home Staging. It had a dramatic, positive impact, not only on the house, but in the lives of the people involved as well. A win-win all the way around!

Shelley Wagner, ASPM, IAHSP
Set the Stage Now
Grosse Pointe Park, Michigan

STAGER GOES THE EXTRA MILE

A real estate agent called. She needed help with a dull and difficult listing. She had heard about "this Staging stuff" from her coworkers at Prudential California Realty, in Benicia, California. She was quite willing to hire a Stager, but there was more than creativity needed here. There were financial difficulties—big ones.

Her seller, recently widowed, was teetering on the edge. With just barely enough money for a new start, she needed to sell. The real estate agent was eager to help her client, but the job at hand was more than she could envision, and the clock was ticking loudly.

(continued)

135

When I got to the home, the first thing the owner did was ask me to remove my shoes. She was over-the-top proud and meticulous about the house—the last project that she and her husband had completed together. They had installed wood-laminate floors, but beyond that, this inconsequential single-level home was in a 1980s time warp.

This was one of the most cooperative sellers I have ever worked with, but she had no idea what to do or where to start. As we toured the house, she was almost immobilized when I suggested that the aquarium on the fake-wood pedestal in the living room should probably be removed. All the while, as we moved from splashy Southwestern style to chrome to country cute, I heard the hum of the air "purifier"—a hot-pink gel mixture next to the fish tank emitting a sickening-sweet scent. With a sweep of her hand, she glowed, as she explained that this was surely a great selling feature!

I felt a tug on my heartstrings when we approached a closed bedroom door. Her mother-in-law was napping, I was told, as she did each day, upon returning from the Alzheimer day care center.

The garage was neatly organized, with a lifetime of accumulations tagged and ready for next weekend's garage sale, an event the seller had deemed necessary to make ends meet these last few months. She was hoping the proceeds from this weekend would pay for my services. Could I help her? Would I? The real estate agent, so sweet and caring, looked as desperate as the seller. "Please," she said.

My goal, I told them, was to meet their budget.

Fast-forward one week—a week consisting of hours spent watering and fertilizing the dying back lawn, replacing light fixtures, and adding greatly to the garage sale inventory. During this week, Southwest was turned into West Coast, and country cute was transformed into comfortable and cozy. The aquarium stayed, but the "aroma dream machine" experienced a sudden power failure. (Oh, darn.)

Near the end of the Staging day, the mother-in-law returned from day care. I was assured that she would go to her room and nap. However, after about 20 minutes, she emerged and followed me around a bit. She asked me if she could help me do anything. I told her no, I was fine. After another 20

(continued)

minutes, she approached me again. I could tell she was feeling unsettled, so I tried to help by suggesting that she fold up the afghans in her room. So off she went to her room.

I finished the Staging and left. I couldn't wait to hear from the agent and the seller. I was even more excited for them to find my statement on the table that said "no charge."

When my phone rang later that night, the seller was in tears—happy tears. She was amazed by the changes. She'd been delayed in calling me because her mother-in-law had been confused by my presence and thought I was moving in. When I left, she thought she had to move out, so she took her neatly folded afghans and a few of her other possessions and put them in a box . . . and walked out the front door! Luckily, some neighbors spied her, took her in, and called the daughter-in-law to pick her up.

The real estate agent's tour was that Friday, and the whole neighborhood was abuzz with interest in this home that was going on the market. One neighbor, at her brother's urging, came right away for a look. Boom! They had a crowded open house! Following this success, the agent got two more listings on that street.

Of course, I saw the sweet seller when I de-Staged. Her whole demeanor had changed and her fear was turning to hope.

Oh, yes, the property sold the first day, before the sun had set, for more than the seller expected. This meant there was enough money to send the mother-in-law to live with her sister back east, and with help from the agent, the seller found a small condominium to call her own. Yes, Staging changes lives.

Linda Jenkins, ASPM, IAHSP
Staging Places
Benicia, California

STAGING RAISES THE BAR

A beautiful 5,000-square-foot home in Sacramento's Del Paso Country Club was set to be listed and sold for $1 million. When I walked in, I saw that the home had only black and white furniture, a dated decor, and an enormous amount of clutter lining hallways and tabletops and cascading out of tubs. The large living room housed not one, but two, grand pianos—one black and one white. The kitchen's impressive granite countertops were buried under a clutter of papers; I didn't even see them at first! The expansive formal dining room was being used as a pseudo-office, with a small drafting table and a chair, while the real office had piles of papers lining the floors and stacked on furniture. A master bedroom with French doors opened to a lovely swimming pool and lawns, but it housed only a massage table and piles of clothes.

The seller knew about Home Staging and had asked his real estate agent to find a professional Stager to work on his home. The house had been updated through the years, and it sat in its colonial grandeur on a beautifully manicured lot across from a golf course. After formulating a plan with the seller, we began our work. To ready the house for sale, I helped the seller find furniture and accessories in warm colors for purchase as well as rental. We packed up clutter and rearranged furniture, eliminating things we knew would not be assets when selling the house (like that massage table in the master bedroom!). We had our work cut out for us. When the house was Staged and listed, it sold for $1.3 million—$300,000 more than the original plan! The seller invested about $30,000 including furniture, decor, and rental and Staging fees, and gained much more in equity and a sold house!

Jennie Norris, ASPM, IAHSP
We Stage Sacramento
Roseville, California

138

ONE HOUSE WAS STAGED, THE OTHER WASN'T: GUESS WHO MADE MORE MONEY?

A real estate agent I work closely with won a listing because he offered Home Staging services, and he was able to negotiate a higher commission percentage as well. The homeowners had a small baby, and one upstairs bedroom was devoted to all the baby things you would expect: a mobile crib, toys, a stroller. Another upstairs room was just papers, everywhere. The living room and dining room were vacant except for a coffee table. The master bedroom was cluttered with lots of extra furniture, including the baby crib and glider. I prepared a detailed written report of what needed to be done prior to the actual hands-on Staging work, and I gave the sellers a deadline of one week to get all their work done.

When the sellers were ready, my team and I returned and spent an afternoon Staging the house for sale. We rearranged furniture, added color with pillows and some carefully chosen artwork, and created appealing groupings in the living and dining rooms. In only four days the house received multiple offers at above list price. Meanwhile, a house down the street with the same floor plan sat on the market, un-Staged and unsold, for two months, and eventually dropped $40,000 in price before attracting a buyer. Wow! What a difference Home Staging makes! The neighbors took notice, and the listing agent for the Staged house received another listing in the same neighborhood strictly because the neighbor saw how quickly the first house had been Staged and sold for the most money in the shortest time!

Jennie Norris, ASPM, IAHSP
We Stage Sacramento
Roseville, California

COMPASSIONATE STAGING

Can I add another C to the Seven C's of Staging? That word would be compassion. I have discovered that Staging is not just about the rewards of the creative process, but also about the rewards that come by honoring people and helping them move on with their lives.

People sell their homes for all kinds of reasons, and when I enter a home to create a product for market, it is with the consent and trust of the homeowner. As an ASP Stager, I have a responsibility not only to be honest and direct, but to do this with compassion. The results can be amazing.

Maria lived in a 6,000-square-foot home that she and her husband had built and where they had raised a family of six children. The house was still full: grandchildren, grown children back home, a retired husband, extended family. The house had been on and off the market for four years. The outside landscaping was overgrown and a broken statue sat on a pad at the dirty front door. There were broken windows, and bordello-red walls and shag carpet in the master bedroom. Kitchen cupboards, once white, were now gray with fingerprints, grease, and scratches. Crystal collections, grandchildren's stuffed animals, and a lifetime of things full of memories were everywhere. When I met Maria she was crippled with arthritis and had to walk backward down the spiral staircase to greet me.

I could tell this job would require work, patience, listening, and compassion, and I was right. We removed red shag carpet, painted walls, cleaned rooms, packed collections, repaired the broken statue, and painted the front door black. It took more than a month to Stage, but Maria's husband and children got on board, and gradually the home evolved into a product. The house went on the market and sold after the first open house! When we went back to pick up our Staging accessories, Maria ran down the stairs frontward! She was free not only of her emotional attachment to the house, but of the crippling arthritis as well. Can you believe it? Just another small Staging miracle. We really do change lives!

Jane Wilson, ASP, IAHSP
Take II Staging Event
Ontario, Canada

GENUINE STAGERS SAVE THE DAY

Here is a great story to show the difference between ASP Stagers and non–ASP Stagers. I got a call to come and look at a house that an interior decorator had "Staged" because the house had not sold after being on the market for almost three months. The list price of the house had dropped by $150,000. We were asked to re-Stage. The Stager wannabes had recommended that the interior be painted, which was good advice, but the colors they had selected were a grayish-blue and tan. The owners had spent $5,000 to have that done, and the colors were wrong. So the first thing we did was customize the wall colors for selling.

The seller, who had already moved to another home, had left the bright-red brick fireplace because he liked it. I shared with him the concept that "buyers only know what they see, not the way it's going to be," explaining to him that by painting out the bricks, the whole room would appear larger. He was still stuck on that red brick fireplace, so I gently reminded him, "You are not living here anymore. Your house is a product on the market, and we need to prepare it for the next owner." He finally got it. By the end of our time together, the sellers were excited about the house and the changes they could make to upgrade its dated look. We recommended paint, new interior doors, baseboards, and some upgrades to the kitchen, along with proper Staging using color and adding warmth.

There was one other issue with the way this house had originally been presented for sale. These "Stagers" had put inventory in the home, but after the house did not sell the first month, they removed all their stuff and returned it to the local Tuesday Morning store, installing 10 modern paintings all over the house. One of their daughters was selling the paintings, so price tags were hanging off each one. I told the sellers and real estate agents that we were selling the house, not the paintings, and furthermore, the paintings were not enhancing the house—there were too many of them, and they were too modern to complement their surroundings.

Coincidentally, my team and I were shopping at Tuesday Morning recently, and when the store manager saw our card, she asked, "Do you normally purchase things and then return them all when you are done?" "No!"

(continued)

141

we vehemently replied. We asked her why she wanted to know about this, and she said that some "home stagers" had done just that (hmmm—sound familiar?) and she was not happy about it. I assured her that I knew of no ASPs who would do something like that. I explained that we are professional businesspeople with ethics, and if we make an inventory purchase, we roll it into one of the many other homes we are Staging. This just goes to show that having a professional designation makes a big difference. Proper training and sound ethics in dealing with other business owners is key.

Jennie Norris, ASPM, IAHSP
We Stage Sacramento
Roseville, California

FROM CLUTTER TO CALM

Jean and Jim had moved to Atlanta in 1985 and bought a 1960s Spanish-style home across from a golf course. When Jim was transferred to Pennsylvania in 2005, they decided to sell the house. Their real estate agent was concerned that the neighborhood had depreciated somewhat, and not much had been done to the house over the past 20 years. She called me in to analyze what needed to be done to market the house.

When I arrived to do the Staging analysis, I could see that some improvements had been made. The bathrooms had recently been updated, and central heating and air-conditioning had been installed to replace radiant heat, but the heating units were still attached to the baseboards. Some interior painting had been done, but it needed refreshing. Jean and Jim would have to do an incredible amount of work to get the house ready to market. The kitchen countertops were the greatest challenge: a do-it-yourselfer had laid inch-square white grouted tiles over bright orange laminate. The backsplash

(continued)

was covered with the same tiles in baby blue. Jean admitted that she was the one who had covered the walls and cabinets with flat canary-yellow wall paint.

Because the kitchen is one of the most important rooms buyers look at, we wanted to give it the facelift it deserved. We worked with a wonderful, creative remodeler who installed granite tiles in place of the old countertops and slate where the baby blues had been. The cabinets were painted with white semigloss, and the walls were painted sage green to match the adjoining breakfast room. The appliances were scrubbed, the hardwood floors polished, and a few accessories added. Voila! A spectacular kitchen emerged. After removing the baseboard heating, the house was repainted inside and out, and all the carpets replaced. A bright mural on the courtyard wall was painted terra cotta, and the fishpond was cleaned and sterilized. Then the Staging magic began. In the expansive living room, a focal-point competition raged between the beautiful natural-stone fireplace and a wonderful view of the courtyard through French doors on the opposite wall. Rearranging the furniture was all it took to welcome guests in through the courtyard to the warmth of the fireplace.

We tackled the four bedrooms next. Again, rearranging the furniture maximized the size of the rooms, and we were off and running. After two months of work, the final art and accessories were put into place, and Staging photos were taken. The house was ready to be marketed for sale.

Six days later, the house sold! The investment to update and Stage the house was close to $20,000, but a very excited and happy Jean and Jim walked away with $250,000 in equity to begin a new life in Pennsylvania.

Wanda Hickman, ASPM, IAHSP
First Impressions
Atlanta, Georgia

TRANSFORMING THE JUNGLE HOUSE

In Wisconsin, I was called in to Stage an old double-decker A-frame house. The sellers had lived there for 23 years and said the carpet had been there before them. The sellers owned a nursery and garden store and would store the live greenery inside the A-frame, which had lofts, balconies, landings, secret rooms, and alcoves. In the area, the house was known as the "Jungle House." The owners had set their sights on a larger home and were eager to get this home sold.

As we toured this miniature castle, I delved through years' worth of precious collectibles, memories, inventory from the garden store, even a wicker box that covered candle drippings on the floor. A jungle of greenery met us at the bottom of the stairs, and vines twined up the banister. One downstairs bedroom was now a storeroom and had been kept closed during earlier showings. The backyard featured a nonfunctioning aboveground pool decorated with graffiti. As we dug through the layers of clutter, newly tiled countertops and other expensive features began to emerge and bloom. Sleeping Beauty was awake!

We Staged every entrance to the house with collections grouped in threes and transformed the storeroom into a quaint guest room retreat. We cleared out the family room so people could walk through easily and created conversation groupings to please potential buyers. The lone bathroom, which also housed a washer and dryer, no longer doubled as towel-and-Tupperware storage. The dining room table, covered for years, sparkled with a newfound shine. The lofts were now clutter free. The "jungle" was relocated into two of the three garages. Old carpets and vines were stripped from the stairwell. At last, the house was Staged and beckoning. The first buyer who came through the front door made an offer, and the contract was secured. It's amazing what creative Staging can do!

Kelly McFrederick, ASPM, IAHSP
Kelly's Staging Kreations
Belle Air, Florida

TELEVISED STAGING

I was asked to do a news segment about Home Staging for Philadelphia's NBC affiliate. They wanted to film local Stagers transforming a house in just 24 hours. I was certainly up for the challenge and asked another ASP if she would like to help me. Of course, she said she would, and after searching for a few weeks, we found a three-bedroom, one-bath, airy row house in a quaint working-class neighborhood of Philly. The family of five was great— all of them living in a 1,012-square-foot home. Needless to say, they were moving to a larger, colonial, single-family home in the suburbs.

When we first entered the house, I knew we had our work cut out for us. With only 24 hours to transform the house into a showplace, it would take every ounce of our creativity! The home was very cluttered and cramped, and we could not even see the dining room table, which was covered literally from end to end.

We did have a comparison house a block away. It had the same floor plan and square footage, except it was a corner lot. It was not Staged and had been on the market for 45 days.

We went into action. We painted three rooms, packed 45 boxes, pulled up carpet in two rooms, put wood restorer on hardwood floors in three rooms, and Staged the entire house. We worked until 11 o'clock that night and started again at 6 o'clock the next morning. When the film crew showed up at 10 A.M., the house looked amazing! The news anchor was astonished by the transformation. She said the house looked totally different. The best part: The house, listed at $125,000, sold in a day for $130,000! Staging is for all properties, from fancy to modest. Staging works!

Brenda Hoover, ASPM, IAHSP
Home Selling Solutions
Hatboro, Pennsylvania

HONORING THE HOMEOWNERS

I recently had the opportunity to help a seller prepare his home for sale, and also help the family heal from a recent loss. This family had lost their father to a terminal illness and then experienced the additional trauma of losing their mother to an extended illness. As you can imagine, because the family had been dealing with both parents' illnesses, hospitalizations, and then deaths, the parents' home had been neglected and became a repository of medical supplies and unanswered mail. The house needed to be sold to settle the estate, but the children were not quite sure where to start. One sibling lived on the opposite coast; the other was a successful salesman who traveled a great deal.

I was contacted by a real estate agent and asked to assist this family with getting the home ready for sale. When I first saw the property I was a little taken aback. The house itself seemed as if it had suffered a long illness. It was dreary, suffocating, and gloomy. Medical supplies and clothing were strewn throughout the bedroom, and months' worth of magazines, personal letters, and newspapers were stacked on the tables. This was not how the parents would have wanted their home to be seen. I wanted to help this family honor their parents by showing their home in a condition they could be proud of. In addition to my typical Staging services, such as a consultation and rearranging the rooms, I helped this family pack and store personal items that were cluttering the home. I found someone to purchase clothing, antiques, and consignment pieces that we didn't need for Staging. I hired a professional cleaning crew to come in and give the home a finishing touch after I was done Staging.

I was able to help this family sell their parents' home within one month of Staging. I know that they felt Staging was essential to making this happen. We not only prepared the home for sale but honored the parents and their possessions as well.

Kate Hart, ASP, IAHSP
Katherine Hart Interiors
Philadelphia, Pennsylvania

STAGING A REHABILITATION

I live on Merritt Island, which is a barrier island off the central east coast of Florida. In September 2004 I bought a house (built in 1984) that was sorely neglected and literally rotting to the ground. Rehabilitating this house was a huge undertaking but also a great opportunity to acquire experience as a future Stager.

I learned of StagedHomes.com from a local newspaper back in June 2005, and I signed up for the November 2005 class in Orlando. That was about the midway point on my house project. I painted walls, removed smelly old carpet and replaced it with laminate wood flooring, and replaced all ceiling fans, light fixtures (adding several chandeliers), every light switch plate, the kitchen sink, and the master bath. And then there was the landscaping! The biggest part of the project was replacing the siding with Hardy Plank and replacing the existing roof with a copper-colored metal one (in the hope it would withstand hurricanes).

This was quite a job, but I was so pleased to have learned from a recent appraisal that in less than 14 months I increased the equity in my home by $130,000. I recently acquired my certificate as an ASP (with intentions of following through with the Masters course sometime in 2006). This is a very exciting time in my life, since I moved to Florida two years ago with no clue of what to do with myself. I cannot wait to see what I can do to help other people earn more equity from their properties!

Terri K. McNeill, ASP
McNeill Stage to Sell, Stage to Live! Inc.
Merritt Island, Florida

SOFTEN TO SELL

It was a typical day in a Stager's life—returning phone calls to real estate agents, shopping, doing research for a project I knew would be upcoming, and later I planned to hop over to the warehouse to log new inventory I had added. As I was working, I received a call from a real estate agent I had never heard of. Our conversation went as follows: "You have a new listing? California Contemporary? (In Texas!, I thought.) Total renovation! You're the third agent to have this listing? Yes, I can meet you there. Thirty minutes—you bet—not a problem!" I drove out and saw that it was an older neighborhood within driving distance of Houston that had seen new interest lately because the golf course was so great. As I rounded the corner and the house came into view, I was taken aback by the unusual design. The real estate agent pulled up, and we exchanged introductions. The exterior of the house had recently been landscaped and, with a few exceptions, had great curb appeal. This house had been built in the 1960s by a film star and it had a very Frank Lloyd Wright look.

As we entered the house I could see right away why it had been on the market for more than a year. All the interior walls and ceilings were either redwood planks, glass, or brick. I'm sure prospective buyers were having a hard time seeing past all those hard surfaces. It was a wonderful house with great architectural design—it just needed softness.

After assessing the house, I prepared a bid and met with the owner. His goal: sell the house! Every day it was on the market was costing him money, and he was prepared to do whatever it took to sell it. I gave him my proposal, which included furnishing the most important rooms, and shared with him this advice: "It is what it is. You don't have to hide it—instead, you run with it." I proposed very contemporary furnishings with bold colors and great art and a few area rugs to help define the areas in the large rooms. Finishing off the room with greenery and lights helped to brighten the space.

(continued)

Wow! What a difference color, lighting, greenery, and fabric made in this house! The real estate agent put the house on a progressive open house tour, and after word got out that this house had been Staged, every agent had to come and see it. Within three weeks, the owner had a contract in his hands. His words to me: "Staging works!"

Judy Taylor, ASPM, IAHSP
Staging Designs of Texas
Montgomery, Texas

THE HOUSE THAT STANDS OUT FROM THE CROWD

One of my key clients had an opportunity to present his real estate services to a potential seller who was thinking of selling his vacant home as For Sale By Owner (FSBO). After the agent explained his marketing plan, which included Home Staging services, he won the listing and arranged for me to meet the seller. I toured the home, took photos, and suggested the seller frame out the windows and doors with trim to help set them off and add visual appeal. The seller and I agreed on a deadline of four days, and when his work was done, the house was Staged by my team. We added color and appeal in all rooms of the house. When we were done, the house looked fabulous and was listed for sale. There were 29 other houses for sale within a five-mile radius. This Staged house received an offer in one week—and when asked why they chose to make an offer on the house, the buyer replied, "It stood out from all the others." Buyers only know what they see, not the way it's going to be!

Jennie Norris, ASPM, IAHSP
We Stage Sacramento
Roseville, California

CHAPTER 11

HOW TO WORK WITH YOUR REAL ESTATE AGENT

A combination of marketing techniques will sell your house. Before your house goes on the market, you will work with your agent to Stage the property so it's in proper showing condition, and then price your house correctly. A good agent will educate you about how he or she works. The more time you spend with your agent before listing your house, the fewer problems you will have down the road. Here's what you can expect and require from your real estate agent as you work together to sell your Staged home.

HOW TO CHOOSE A LISTING AGENT

There are so many listing agents, and you have to pick one to do the job. How do you choose? You want an agent you have rapport with, who understands you and your home, and who is committed to getting you a good price and a speedy sale. Your listing agent should be a marketing expert who will encourage as many agents as possible to bring their buyers through your house. Most of your agent's marketing efforts will target other agents, who will see your house on tours with other agents from their office, in the multiple listings, and at brokers' open houses. Get to know a few agents, see what each has to offer, and ask how much time and energy they'll devote to your house. Let's say an area has 2,000 working agents, and 25 agents come to a brokers' open house. One agent may consider that open house a success, but I'd say that 1,975 agents have not yet seen your house. Ask how many brokers' open houses your agent can promise you.

In truth, your listing agent will probably not be the agent ("the selling agent") who ultimately brings the buyer through your front door. Statistics from the multiple listing services show this to be true. But your agent will be responsible for the outreach and marketing that make your home so appealing. When all is said and done, you will feel that your agent is truly the one who sold your house. Even if another agent brings in a purchaser, a good agent will work with the selling agent to help the buyer qualify for financing and move the sale to completion. Your agent should be up to date on all the current financing programs available, to help purchasers find the best deal possible.

Most important, you want an agent who is a closer. You want your house to sell, with no slipups that might delay or kill the sale at the very end; that's just too disappointing, after all the work it takes to sell a house. As an agent, I can tell you that I have driven three hours to another city at midnight because a bank forgot to have a purchaser sign three additional documents, and then I've turned around and driven at half past two in the morning to another city to deliver those papers to an escrow officer at her own home. The sale closed on time, and it wouldn't have happened otherwise. Your agent should be committed to doing everything possible—as long as it is legal, moral, and ethical—to close the sale. Your agent will follow the banker, attorney, escrow people, and inspectors to be sure the transaction closes. (In some parts of the country, a closing is called a *settlement*.)

ARE YOU GETTING ALL YOU DESERVE FROM YOUR REAL ESTATE AGENT?

As a real estate agent myself, and as the creator of Home Staging and the Accredited Staging Professional designation, I can tell you what to expect when you work with a real estate agent.

A real estate agent should meet with you and get to know your house from top to bottom, inside and out. An agent can create a marketing program to sell your house in the best way possible, leveraging all its pluses to get you a fast sale and a high price. You, in turn, need to be committed to selling your house and be willing to make the changes and improvements your agent recommends so that your property goes on the market in top shape, and properly priced.

You want an agent you have good rapport with—someone you can like and trust. A good agent does more than put a sign on your lawn and an ad in the paper. You are paying that agent to market and sell your house; you want to know what the agent has in mind for your house. Together, you are a team, working together toward a common goal: a fast and profitable sale.

Good real estate agents will

- Tell you who they are, what they do, and how they do it.
- Explain what makes their service different from that of other agents.
- Get to know you and find out why you are selling, so they can help you price your house correctly and prepare it for sale.
- Explain the services they will provide for you, the seller, by preparing a detailed report of what they will do to market and sell your property, along with a pricing analysis, called a *comparative market analysis* (CMA), comparing your home with others on the market at the same time.
- Educate you about pricing, Staging, and marketing your house.

Owners make the ultimate decision on their home's selling price, and an agent's job is to give sellers an honest, professional opinion of where their house fits in today's market. The agent will advise you about price and terms, such as special financing or buyers' warranties, that can help to sell your house.

After you meet the agent and show your property, you should expect a return visit, at which point the agent will outline his or her marketing plans for your home. Good agents will tell you about their company—its history, awards, and services—and also let you know about the work they have done individually at the company to sell properties in the most effective way possible. You want the hardest worker and the most attentive agent marketing your property.

Both the sellers and their agent complete the paperwork to put the home on the market. The agent should show you a copy of the listing agreement that the multiple listing service (MLS) in your area uses, or your agent's company may have its own forms.

Every agent in the surrounding area will know your house is for sale because it is listed in the MLS—often referred to as "the multiple"—which is available to agents via the Internet. An agent should show you how your home will be featured in the MLS and tell you how far the MLS region extends by showing you a map of your area.

When your house is on the market, the agent will set up an information center in your home, often in the foyer or on the dining room table, with a stack of information sheets about the home, the agent's business card, and a bowl or tray where visiting agents will drop their cards when they show the house. Ask to see samples of the information sheets that will go inside and outside your home for buyers to look at. These should be high quality, with crisp pictures and a dynamic description of the unique features and special aspects of your house, including special financing or buyer's warranties, with everything spelled correctly.

Some agents will also prepare a booklet about your home, providing information about the schools, churches, recreation, shopping, parks, and athletic fields. This may include your home's heating and cooling costs, blueprints, plat maps, and landscaping plans. All this information makes it easier for buyers to decide to buy your house.

Your agent should go through the property with you and

suggest how to Stage your house for sale, inside and out. This is crucial, and you should expect nothing less. You should be there to take the agent through the property, so you can talk about the home's special features. It's important that everyone is on board to sell the property and understands the selling price and the marketing efforts that will be undertaken to sell the property at that price. In a slow market, this marketing, including Staging, will help sell your property faster. In a hot market, Staging can help sell your house quickly, usually for more money.

FILLING OUT ALL THOSE FORMS

It's helpful to familiarize yourself ahead of time with the forms used in the sale and closing of your house. Your agent should be able to show you the paperwork for the purchase and sale agreement, as well as a financing rate sheet from a local lender, title insurance information, a sample inspection report and a sample appraisal report, and a blank deed form. There are particular steps that must be taken to close a sale, and you should be familiar with these as well.

Don't be surprised if your listing agent asks you to sign a request to verify information about your current loan, which will come from your bank or mortgage company. The agent needs your signature to get information in writing from the lending institution about the financing on your present home. The listing agent needs to know all the facts about your current loan so things go smoothly at the closing.

QUESTIONS FOR YOUR REAL ESTATE AGENT

It's reasonable to ask agents for answers to the following questions. By comparing their answers, you can choose an agent who is right for you.

What services do you offer?

What is your range of fees?

What is your success record?

How long does it take for your listings to sell?

What is your recommendation for a selling price?

What are the asking prices of nearby homes currently for sale?

Can you show us the written comparative market analysis of recent selling prices for neighborhood homes?

Can you supply references from three sellers you have worked with recently?

Will you bring the other agents in your office to see my house? This usually happens the first Monday or Tuesday after you have Staged your house for sale. Remember, agents, like buyers, remember only what they see, not the way it's going to be. Make sure your house looks its best this day, and forever after, while it's on the market. Agents typically go on a caravan each week to see the houses just listed on the market.

Will you conduct a brokers' open house at my house?

Do you plan on having a public open house at my house?

Do you create and distribute a flyer about my house to other agents in the MLS? When I was an active real estate agent, I made it a practice to send flyers about each of my properties to each agent in my MLS area. Yes, that means a lot of flyers, but it also means that lots and lots of people know the houses I have for sale. Remember, the real estate business is a business of communication and cooperation. I would rather have another agent sell one of my listings quickly (both of us make money, and the sellers get their equity) than have that property sit, waiting for me to sell it by myself.

Do you provide a written report of the ongoing work you are doing to sell my house?

REAL ESTATE ETIQUETTE

Do use your real estate agent as an intermediary to communicate anything to other buyers or sellers. Always work through your agent.

Don't visit the house you're in contract to buy without your real estate agent accompanying you. Real estate etiquette calls for you to notify the present homeowner before stepping onto the property for any reason, during that in-between time after the house is in contract but before the closing. Do not bring the septic tank cleaner, the curtain maker, the tennis court maintenance person, or the pool guy to the house without making those arrangements through your agent and the seller's agent. Of course, the present homeowner always has the right to say no to any of these visits, but generally people are amenable if you work through the proper channels.

Don't see a buyer with a purchase and sale agreement

without your listing agent being present. If an agent calls and says she has a buyer for your house, refer the agent to your listing agent. Don't sign anything without your listing agent right beside you. Once you sign, your agreement is set in stone. Don't sign without proper counsel.

ABOUT ADVERTISING

All sellers like to see their house advertised in the newspaper. It makes them feel good because the company has chosen their home to feature to the world. Ads make the company telephone ring and bring purchasers to the company. But in truth, less than 4 percent of homes are sold from ads. Ads don't sell houses; agents do. Most houses are sold because an agent brought a qualified buyer to show the home and then sold it. As a seller, recognize that ads are good, but ultimately it's the traffic through your home that will most likely sell your house.

CHAPTER 12

HOW HOME STAGING IS CHANGING THE REAL ESTATE INDUSTRY

The real estate industry is changing in a big way. I have seen these changes coming, and so far my predictions have played out correctly. Since I first came up with the concept of Home Staging in the early 1970s, I have predicted the very powerful changes and the impact Home Staging is bringing to the real estate industry. I want to share those changes with you and share more forecasts for the future of the real estate industry and the future of Home Staging.

I always talk about the ingredients of a sale: location, condition, price, terms available, the state of the market, and Home Staging. I believe Home Staging has the biggest impact of all. Traditionally, people always say, "Location, location, location." Well, location is very important and does affect the price, but Home Staging affects the price in *any* location. Market conditions affect all properties, and with all things being relative,

Staged homes have the edge. A Staged property sells more quickly and for more money, even when the location is not the best. I know and believe that Home Staging is the most important factor in selling a house.

How can that be, you ask? Well, each area of a city has its own price range. Therefore, in any market, in any price range, for that area of the city or town, a Staged home will look better than the others and thus will sell faster and for more money.

Home Staging works no matter what the market is doing or where interest rates are going. Staging allows sellers to find the best buyer for their property, and allows buyers to choose a much more attractive property. People love living in a Staged home because it's a less stressful environment.

When I Staged a house on ABC's *20/20,* the host, John Stossel, asked a representative of the National Association of Realtors about the value of the services real estate agents provide to the seller. Now, as you read my predictions here, please bear in mind that I am a real estate agent and an affiliate real estate agent, and I have sold more than 3,000 homes as a real estate agent as well. I believe in the real estate industry, in being a real estate agent, and in being a member of the National Association of Realtors. But each real estate agent runs his or her business differently. In my business, I always insisted that my clients have their homes prepared for sale by having them Staged. This provides a client with the highest level of service for the good of all concerned. Many real estate agents don't do this. They don't educate their clients about why they should Stage their homes. I liken this to a doctor who backs down on a blood test if a patient is afraid to have blood taken. No doctor I know of would do that, yet agents practice real estate this way all the time. If the agent doesn't insist that a seller Stage their house, the house often sits without offers to buy and/or doesn't sell for as much as it could have.

However, when a Staged home sells, everyone benefits. The homeowner sells quickly and gets the most money. The buyers can see what they're buying and easily move in. It's easier for the mortgage company to lend money on a good-looking house that's Staged, and the house is easily appraised—and sometimes for a higher value. The title company has a better-looking home to insure, the escrow company has fewer problems closing the sale, and with the sold Staged home as a comparable, the whole neighborhood benefits from the increased property value that is established. All this activity supports the real estate market, which affects and supports the economy.

Where is all this heading? What changes do I predict for the future of Home Staging and the real estate industry? This is what I see:

1. *The ASP Home Stager will help set the market and begin the home selling process even before the real estate agent gets involved.* The public will begin to call Home Stagers before they call real estate agents. This has a huge impact on the real estate industry. When the seller finds out what a difference Home Staging makes in selling a home, he or she will want to Stage it before listing it for sale—wouldn't you? (To learn more, visit our web site at www.StagedHomes.com, where you can also hear my radio show.)

Staging is a marketing tool. Staging is merchandising. Staging is setting the best scene so the buyer sees the features of the house in the best light possible. A spotless, uncluttered Staged home done in appropriate colors helps the buyer visualize living there—and no one buys a home until they can see themselves living there. No one. Even investment and commercial properties need to be Staged so potential owners and tenants can visualize the space in its best light.

Do you realize what a shift in perspective this is? Sellers have always called their real estate agents first and then expected them to sell the house with an ad, a public open house, a brokers' open house—the usual routine. As a top agent, I know it takes a whole lot of creative marketing to sell a house and give the very best service to the seller. So it's revolutionary when the public calls the ASP Home Stager first.

It changes the decades-old practices of the real estate industry and can even turn them upside down. It is already happening. For the past year at StagedHomes.com, almost half the traffic on our web site has looked for an ASP Home Stager before looking for a real estate agent to list their house for sale. Real estate agents might feel threatened by Stagers—at least some of them do. When it comes to the line of service, they like to be in first position with sellers. One concern of real estate agents might be that the Stager will refer the seller to another agent instead.

When sellers tell their real estate agent that they are considering or have contacted a Stager, many agents balk, saying, "Oh, you don't need to do that; your house is fine the way it is." This makes the agent look out of date, because an agent's goal is always to sell a home for top dollar. In truth, an agent should always refer a seller to an ASP Stager. Having the house Staged means the seller will usually receive more equity and will certainly sell in a shorter amount of time. Both the agent and the seller receive more money when the house sells for a higher price.

Too many agents think "little picture" instead of "big picture" when they list and sell properties. Some other agents are simply uninformed about the benefits of Staging. In the real estate business, 80 percent of the business is done by 20 percent of the agents, and they usually have the best interests of the sellers at heart. The other 80 percent of the agents may or may not have the sellers' best interests in first place. They may just want to sell and move on to another listing. Some may feel that houses sell fast in their area, so there's no need to Stage.

All these years, I have conducted my real estate and Home Staging business knowing that as I help others achieve their goals, my goals will be taken care of, too. In a choice among service, ego, and money, service should always come first. When you serve others first, your income will take care of itself and will be there for you in the end.

2. *Everyone's role is important.* What is needed now (and, believe me, I am working on it!) is a fresh approach that will educate everyone involved in the real estate industry.

Real estate agents need to be educated and certified as ASP real estate agents so they can teach sellers the benefits of Home Staging. Anyone who is selling a house should have that home Staged.

Then, the ASP real estate agent needs to team up with an ASP Stager. Every real estate agent should have an ASP Stager on his or her team. The ASP real estate agent refers the seller to the ASP Stager, who prepares the home for sale with the seller. Agents don't have time to Stage a house. Working to sell a house and finding the right home for a buyer is a full-time job in itself.

Agents don't do home inspections or appraisals; they farm those services out to the experts. In the same way, they delegate

Staging to a trained ASP Stager, who knows how to complete the job the right way. ASP Stagers work full-time to prepare homes for sale, and they have been trained to do so in my ASP Home Staging courses. As the creator of Home Staging, I have devoted my life to this mission, and I can promise you that ASP Stagers know their business and know how to do it right. ASP Stagers know how to communicate with the client so the Home Staging is done correctly. It is crucial that agents and Stagers team up and work together to give the very best service to the seller. With teamwork, everyone wins—especially the people who are buying and selling the Staged home.

3. *Commissions and fees may change.* Here's a typical scenario: You decide to sell your house. You find an agent. Maybe the agent marketed himself or herself in your neighborhood. Maybe you saw an ad or a friend referred you. Or you have known this agent for a number of years. You list your house with this agent for $500,000 and agree to pay the agent, for example, a 5, 6, or 7 percent commission. (Remember, all commissions are negotiable.) The agent says he or she will advertise your house for sale in a local newspaper or magazine. The agent will put up the For Sale sign, make brochures about your house, and install a lockbox or key safe so other agents can show your house. The agent shows you a marketing plan—and in writing (which you should insist on). The agent also introduces you to a trained Accredited Staging Professional (an ASP) and suggests that you prepare your home for sale. Or maybe you found an ASP Stager on our StagedHomes.com web site and the ASP referred you to an ASP real estate agent. So far, so good.

You pay the Stager $3,500 to Stage the house, and two days later the house sells. That's good news. But you start to think, "Well, let's see here . . . I am paying the agent a $30,000 commission and I paid the ASP Stager $3,500. The house sold right away, for top dollar. There wasn't time for the agent to write an ad or hold an open house. No office tour or brokers' open house took place. Actually, not much marketing had to be done because the ASP Stager did such a great job."

4. *Should the real estate agent pay the ASP Stager's fee?* Sellers, ask yourself this question: Are the fees you're paying fair and balanced? It's great that the agent put you into the multiple listing service and put the sign up, but maybe it was the Staging that sold the house for more money. Maybe the agent should have paid the Stager. Maybe the Stager should have gotten a bit more and the agent a bit less. Who is really getting the house sold? Why should the seller be the one to pay for the Stager when it's the agent's job to market the house, and Staging is part of the marketing?

It is wonderful that the agent introduced you to the ASP Stager, but I think it was the Staging that made the difference. There was no need to market the house further: It sold! You got the price you wanted.

These are the kinds of questions a homeowner starts to ask when they decide to sell their house.

5. *The real estate agent is crucial!* As a real estate agent myself, I feel it's crucial to point out that a seller pays an agent for a lot more than just securing a buyer. A seller pays an agent to *close* the sale. *This point must never be forgotten!* Many challenges can arise after the buyer and seller have signed

the purchase and sale agreement. The home inspection may show dry rot on the deck. The buyer may have a problem with his or her credit score. These are issues for the agent. Staging has nothing to do with the condition of the house and should never cover up any defects in the house. Staging sets the scene and ensures that the house is clean and clutter free, and the right colors have been used throughout.

Those real estate agents who have ASP Stagers on their team will become the leaders of the real estate industry in every market in every city. There is a huge difference between generic Staging and ASP Staging. Every day ASP Stagers are called to de-Stage and re-Stage work done by so-called Stagers who aren't ASPs. ASP Stagers are trained in the standards, ethics, guidelines, procedures, skills, and policies of Home Staging before they are qualified as Accredited Staging Professionals. The difference is easy to see.

6. *Always hire an ASP Stager to Stage a home.* Anybody can wake up and say, "Well, today I think I will become a Stager." But it could be a huge mistake for a seller or real estate agent to hire a Stager who has no training. Make sure your Home Stager is an accredited ASP. It *is* the credential you can count on. ASP Staging is the only kind of Home Staging you should do. The marketing services that real estate agents provide to sellers should always include referring or bringing in an ASP Stager. This ensures that the Staging is done correctly, and that the sellers get their homes sold for top dollar in any marketplace.

Education is the power behind an ASP Stager and the whole Home Staging industry, which I invented, developed, and have grown since 1972. ASPs work with the guidelines to do it right.

ASPs stand above all the rest. Insist that your home be Staged by an ASP. Insist that your real estate agent use or refer you to an ASP Home Stager. This is the benchmark designation of the Home Staging industry. And make sure that you list your home with an ASP real estate agent, as well.

7. *ASP Stagers and ASP real estate agents work together as teams.* If real estate agents and their companies want to maintain their fee structure, they need to become more responsible for marketing houses by having an ASP Stager on their team. Not only should they refer the ASP Stager, they should also pay for the ASP Stager by making Staging part of their marketing budget. When you're selling your house, insist on an ASP Stager and an ASP real estate agent. That way you will have the best team in the industry.

When ASP real estate agents and ASP Stagers work together, they can offer you the highest level of service, and will assist each other in serving your wants and needs to help you reach your goals.

It's all about presentation. Today's world runs on presentation. TV is Staged. Radio is Staged. Movies are Staged. Politics is Staged. Advertising is Staged. The whole world is a Stage—and your life is, too.

8. *The Home Staging industry will grow larger each year.* When a good thing starts happening, you can't stop it. That's what's happening with Home Staging. When you Stage your house for sale and it sells quickly for more money, you'll want to Stage every house you sell thereafter. You will also want to Stage to Live, because a clean house without clutter that's painted in soothing colors is a less stressful environment. This

cultural shift is taking place now and will be seen and felt in many ways. Many people won't pay to have their homes decorated; often, there's simply not enough motivation to have it done. But once sellers feel the impact of living in a Staged home while it is on the market, they want to live in a Staged home all the time.

9. *The earning potential for the Home Staging industry is huge.* Think about becoming an ASP Stager as a career. If this is of interest to you, you can do it. It is exciting to own and build your own Accredited Home Staging business, and you'll have the time of your life doing so. The stories in this book and the quotes from sellers, ASP Stagers, and ASP real estate agents offer just a taste of the wonderful things that happen when homes are Staged.

Real estate agents who work hard earn a very good income, and so do ASP Home Stagers. And you don't have to go out and buy a whole store to become an ASP Stager. In fact, I don't think you should. You can rent furniture and accessories that the seller pays for, or you can rent out your own inventory over and over again. I'd rather see ASP Stagers earn their fees by using their creativity, rather than just by selling things. Creativity is where the fun is. Creativity and service are what make an ASP Stager stand out from the crowd. Anyone can sell someone a truckload of furniture. But remember, Home Staging is not decorating. You have read about the differences here in this book. Years ago I had a decorating business, and you couldn't pay me to go back to it—too many headaches. Home Staging is fun. Home Staging feeds my creativity in a way decorating homes never could. Working within a particular budget and time frame, you make a home look its best, using things the seller already owns. It's similar to setting the stage in the theater or the movies. That's why I named this business "Staging" in the first place. The goals are the same: You set the scene, set the Stage, play to a sellout crowd, and the audience falls in love with the production.

Retailers are just awakening to the huge growth potential the Home Staging industry offers. It involves stores, products, ideas, and financial programs such as the Home Advantage Credit Card, which lets you "Stage It Now and Pay for It Later." The card is for ASP real estate agents, sellers, and ASP Stagers; for details, visit www.HomeAdvantageCard.com. Using the card, you can earn reward points to help pay down the principal balance on your mortgage. What a concept! This has never been done before.

10. *Sellers will have their homes Staged, and those homes will sell for top dollar.* Home Staging is spreading around the world. Right now, homes are being Staged in the United States, Canada, Hungary, Ireland, England, Australia, Sweden, and other countries, too. When I started this industry back in 1972, little did I know that I had started a wave that would travel around the world. And I have a special keepsake with me to help me stay the course. In 1985, a minister who became a real estate agent attended one of my earliest real estate training sessions. After the training, he gave me a note on a beautiful card. He had written: "Barb, I think you have a message that will one day spread around the world. Barb, you have a message the world needs to hear." I have never forgotten this note. That card and his message have helped me hold to my vision many

times over the years. I have stayed true to my mission, which is to bring Home Staging to all the places people call home, all around the world. I thank the man who wrote those encouraging words, and the spirit behind his words.

Thank you for spreading the word about Home Staging. My dream is happening right before my eyes. Thank you for reading my book. In doing so, you become part of my dream, too.

STAGING RESOURCE CENTER

RECIPE FOR A SALE

Six key elements will influence the sale of your home. When all these ingredients are positive, you have a sale! If just one of them is out of line, it will take longer to sell your property. If several are out of line, expect your home to remain on the market longer. Staging is a powerful selling tool that can speed the purchase of your home and raise its selling price.

1. *Home Staging.* Homes that are prepared for sale sell quicker and/or for more money. Staging will immediately give your property an edge in any market.
2. *Price.* Price is so important in the sale of a home. A property is really only worth what one person is willing to pay another to gain ownership. Price must be in direct relationship to the other key elements for a sale and is the most important factor of all.
3. *Location.* Appraisers always say "location, location, location," and it's true. The price of your home must reflect its location.
4. *Condition.* To obtain the highest value for your home, it should be in good condition and be well maintained. Your price must reflect the condition of the home.

5. *Terms.* The more terms available on your property, the more potential buyers you can reach. Your price must reflect the kind of terms available to purchase it, such as special financing or warranties offered to the buyers.

6. *The market.* Interest rates, competition, and the economy influence the state of the market, and the pricing of your property must reflect the current status of the market.

Copyright © 2006 StagedHomes.com.

WHY SHOULD YOU STAGE YOUR HOME?

Your Staged home will look better than similar homes, allowing it to sell faster and/or for more money.

- Because your home has been professionally Staged, it will be recognized as a Staged home.
- A Staged home will look better than competing homes for sale in your local market, allowing you to sell faster and/or for more money.
- Staged homes are recognized by other real estate agents as properties ready to sell, and therefore are more likely to be shown to potential buyers.
- Staged homes are recognized by buyers as the best properties to see.
- More buyers want to see Staged homes, increasing your visibility and showings.
- Staged homes qualify for special promotional materials including street signs and print material designations, allowing your home to be marketed to more potential buyers.

Copyright © 2006 StagedHomes.com.

YOUR PERSONAL MOVING CHECKLIST

Moving does take lots of time and energy, and it can be a stressful experience for some people. Use this list. It will definitely help. There is no substitute for good planning. Plan ahead! Roll with the punches, and things will go more smoothly. Try to relax and enjoy the adventure.

SIX WEEKS BEFORE MOVING

- Make an inventory of everything to be moved.
- Collect everything you're not taking with you for a garage sale or charity.
- Contact the charity for date/time of pickup. Save receipts for tax records.
- Contact several moving companies for estimates.
- Select a mover; arrange for the exact form of payment at the destination (cash, check, cashier's check or money order).
- Get cartons and packing materials to start packing *now*.

- Contact your insurance agent to transfer or cancel coverage.
- Check with your employer to find out what moving expenses they will pay.

FOUR WEEKS BEFORE MOVING

- Notify all magazines of your change of address.
- Check with your veterinarian for pet records and immunizations.
- Contact utility companies for refunds of deposits; set a turnoff date.
- Dry-clean clothes to be moved; pack them in protective wrappers.
- Collect everything you have loaned out; return everything you have borrowed.
- Service power mowers, boats, snowmobiles, and so forth, that are to be moved. Drain all gas/oil to prevent fire in the moving van.
- Check with doctors and dentist for all family records and prescriptions.
- Get children's school records.
- Check the freezer and plan to use the food over the next two to three weeks.
- Remove all jewelry and other valuables to a safe-deposit box or other safe place to prevent loss during the move.
- Give away or arrange for transportation of houseplants (most moving companies will *not* move plants, especially

in winter). Plants can also be sold at garage sales or make perfect thank-you gifts for neighbors.

ONE WEEK BEFORE MOVING

- Transfer or close checking and savings accounts. Arrange for a cashier's check or money order to pay the moving company on arrival in your new community.
- Have your automobile serviced for the trip.
- Fill out post office change-of-address forms; give them to the postmaster.
- Check and make an inventory of all furniture for dents and scratches; notify the moving company of your inventory and compare on arrival at your new house.
- Dispose of all combustibles and spray cans. (Spray cans can explode or burn—don't pack them.)
- Pack a separate carton of cleaning utensils and tools (screwdriver, hammer, etc.).
- Separate cartons and luggage you need for personal/ family travel—everything that stays with you and won't go with the moving van.
- As you pack, mark each box with the name of the room it will be going to in your new home.
- Organize at least one room in the house in which packers and movers can work freely.
- Cancel all newspapers, garden service, and the like.
- Review this entire list to make certain that you haven't overlooked anything.

MOVING DAY

- Plan to spend the entire day at the house you've sold. Last-minute decisions must be made by you.
- Don't leave until after the movers have gone.
- Hire a babysitter or send the children to a friend's house for the day.
- Stay with the moving van driver to oversee the inventory.
- Tell packers and/or the driver about fragile or precious items.
- Make a final check of the entire house—basement, closets, shelves, attic, garage—every room.
- Approve and sign the bill of lading. If possible, accompany the driver to the weigh station.
- Double-check with the driver to make certain moving company records show the proper delivery address for your new house. Verify the scheduled delivery date as well.
- Give the driver phone and cell phone numbers both here and in your new community so the company can contact you in case of a problem.
- Get complete routing information and phone numbers from the driver so you can call the driver or company in case of an emergency en route.
- Lock all the doors and windows. Advise your real estate agent and neighbors that the house is empty.

Copyright © 2006 StagedHomes.com.

BARB SCHWARZ'S HOME STAGING WISDOM: WORDS THAT WORK

"Clutter eats equity!"

"You can't sell it if you can't see it."

"The investment in Staging your home is less than your first price reduction!"

"Start packing because you'll be moving."

"If you can smell it, you can't sell it."

"Would you consider selling a car without touching up the chips, washing/waxing it, vacuuming it for each showing, and fixing any problems? Many sellers on the market have not even done that with their own homes. They haven't gotten them ready to sell. *Detail your house like you detail your car.*"

"The way you live in a home and the way you sell your house are two different things."

"You are earning yourself money with the time and energy you invest getting your home ready for sale."

"By preparing your home for sale, you will be so much further ahead of the competition."

"The Seven C's of Staging—Clean, Clutter free, Color, Compromise, Creativity, Commitment, Communication."

"Your home becomes a house and your house becomes a product for sale on the open market, and the public will be coming through."

"Staging is a marketing tool."

"Buyers, agents, and appraisers only know what they see, not the way it's going to be!"

"Staging is the picture frame and mat on the picture, and the picture is the house."

PRICING AND SELLING YOUR STAGED HOME

"Don't just put your house on the market and 'see' what happens. Stage it to sell!"

"There is no *try,* only *do.*"

"If you are too high in price, the other agents won't show your house, but if you are being shown and you are not getting a purchase and sale agreement, then the buyers think you are overpriced compared to the competition they are seeing!"

"Location, condition, price, terms, the state of the market, and Staging—these are the six main factors that sell homes, and of these, price is the most influential, based on the other five."

"The best time to sell a home is in the first three weeks!"

"When homes are listed on the market, some are always used to sell others. Those homes are called 'comparables.' I don't want your home to be a comparable, I want it to sell!"

"Most qualified buyers are working with real estate agents."

Copyright © 2006 StagedHomes.com.

WHO IS AN ACCREDITED STAGING PROFESSIONAL?

An *Accredited Staging Professional* (ASP) is a dedicated professional who has studied and learned the proven and powerful techniques of *Staging* homes.

An *Accredited Staging Professional* (ASP) has successfully completed a detailed ASP course on preparing homes for sale.

An *Accredited Staging Professional* (ASP) will Stage your house so it looks better than the competition by being clean, clutter free, and ready to show to prospective buyers.

An *Accredited Staging Professional* (ASP) is committed to the principles and practices of marketing properties as *Staged* homes.

To find an ASP in your area, go to www.StagedHomes.com.

Copyright © 2006 StagedHomes.com.

WHAT YOU CAN EXPECT IF YOU WORK WITH AN ACCREDITED STAGING PROFESSIONAL

Accredited Staging Professionals (ASPs) abide by a code of ethics.

> They believe in their ability to help clients Stage their properties.
>
> They follow and protect their code of ethics for the good of all Accredited Staging Professionals (ASPs).
>
> They establish and maintain professional policies. They hold their clients accountable to prepare their homes for sale and keep them in Staged showing condition until the home is sold and the inspection and appraisal are completed.
>
> They protect the quality of Staging by following the Staging criteria and use the word "Staged" only to describe homes that have truly met or exceeded those criteria.

They display and market their ASP designation in their Staging marketing materials to inform people that they are an Accredited Staging Professional.

They educate their clients and the public as to the meaning and origin of Staging to enhance the ASP designation for all ASPs.

They bring credit to the ASP designation through their honesty, their integrity, and by honoring their clients and themselves.

Copyright © 2006 StagedHomes.com.

BARB SCHWARZ'S STAGING CRITERIA

When you get ready to place a home on the market for sale it becomes a product, and just like any product on the shelves at your local store, it has features and benefits, pluses and minuses, and there are other products to compete with. To gain an edge in your marketplace your house must be priced right and look better than the competition. Sometimes it's difficult to think of a home as a mere product, but it helps to think that way so that you can get top dollar for your property and sell it in a reasonable amount of time.

When you sell your home, you're going to have to move. When you move, you're going to have to pack. And when you Stage, you're going to pack up some of your things early. It's a little bit of work, but you're going to have to do it anyway, so let's do it now so you can get top dollar for your property in your marketplace. Here's a review of important Staging steps.

GENERAL GUIDELINES

☐ In every room, stand at the doorway and look at the room through the eyes of a buyer. What do you see? Be tough on yourself: What can you live without while your home is on the market?

☐ Most carpets need to be cleaned. Have them profession- ally cleaned before putting your home on the market. *Buyers only know what they see, not the way it's going to be!* Unless your home is a fixer-upper, badly worn or very out-of-date carpets should be replaced before putting your home on the market. Offering buyers a credit to pick their own new carpet or a discount off the price is far less effective and will always end up costing you more money and slow the selling process. Pick a light-colored short plush or Berber carpet. "Real estate beige" is the safest color.

☐ Check all light fixtures. Are they working properly? Replace all burned-out lightbulbs. Look for dark hallways and cor- ners and increase the wattage of bulbs in those areas.

"The way you live in your home and the way you market and sell your house are two different things!"

—Barb Schwarz

☐ Make sure there are lamps with adequate bulbs in dark cor- ners that are turned on for showings.

☐ Repair and repaint cracks on all walls and ceilings.

☐ Repair or replace broken light switches and switch plates. Clean any dirty areas around them.

☐ Keep all curtains and blinds open during the day to let in light and views. The extra cost of additional heating or air- conditioning is a necessary cost of selling.

☐ Reduce the number of pillows on couches to zero, one, three, or five. Remove all afghans and blankets.

☐ Pack up all valuable items to protect them. If necessary, take them to a safe-deposit box.

☐ Take a hard look at your beloved houseplants. In most cases they need to be pruned and/or the number of plants reduced to create more space. If plants don't look healthy and are just barely clinging to life, give them away.

☐ Fireplaces need to be cleaned out. Glass doors should be cleaned. Mantels and hearths need to be cleared off except for a very few necessary items.

☐ To create more space, you may want to remove a chair, a love seat, or other pieces of furniture.

☐ Pack up all collections. (You're going to need to pack them up sooner or later, anyway.) They become a distraction for buyers from the desired focal point—your home.

☐ Reduce the number of books on bookshelves. Pack up extra books early!

☐ Eliminate family pictures on shelves, pianos, and tables.

☐ Reduce the number of wall-hung photos and paintings in every room to one large piece on a wall or a small group of three. Make sure they are hung at eye level.

☐ Keep soft music playing at all times for showings—easy listening or light jazz, not hard rock or funeral music.

☐ Be sensitive to odors, because buyers are! Excessive cooking or smoking odors, dog or cat odors, baby, laundry, and mildew odors will turn off buyers. If there is a challenge with odors in your home, use room deodorants or disinfectant sprays and keep windows cracked open for ventilation even in very hot or cold weather. (There are great products in pet stores for pet odors, and many professional carpet cleaners have special ozone machines that can really help with difficult odors.) *You can't sell it if you can smell it!*

☐ Wash all windows and make sure they operate freely. If the seal is broken on a double-pane window, replace it now.

☐ Repair items that are broken. This will show that your home is well taken care of. In most cases, buyers will ask for them to be repaired anyway, so do it now.

☐ Don't be afraid to move furniture from room to room. That extra chair from the living room or dining room may just look great in the master bedroom.

☐ In general, pack up the little things. Little things create clutter and they need to be packed up anyway, so pack them up now.

INSIDE THE HOME

LIVING ROOM, FAMILY ROOM, DEN, BONUS ROOM, OR REC ROOM

If you go into a model home that is newly constructed, you will see that it is usually sparsely decorated. In a resale home, you need to create space for buyers to mentally move into the room by reducing clutter and the overall number of items.

☐ Clear off all coffee tables and end tables and leave just two or three magazines and one nice vase or piece of statuary.

☐ Remove all ashtrays.

DINING ROOM

☐ Clear off the dining room table except for one nice centerpiece.

☐ Remove the tablecloth if the table is spectacular.

☐ Remove extra leaves from the table to make the room look bigger.

☐ Remove extra dining room chairs if they crowd the table or fill up the corners of the room. Four or six chairs are plenty. It will make the room look bigger, and you can put the extra chairs in the garage or a storage unit.

☐ Remove or reduce the number of items, valuable items, and collections, as in the living room. The same rules apply here, too, especially in a sideboard or buffet.

KITCHEN

The main question in the kitchen is: What can you live without? Clear off counters, leaving only a very few items that you have to use on a daily basis. Everything else should be kept off the counters to create space. Most homes have far too many small appliances and other items out that should be stored out of sight. Leave out a few large decorative items such as a bowl of fruit or a basket with bread in it.

☐ Repair any tile or Formica countertops and edges that have been damaged or come unglued.

☐ Clean tile grout with bleach if it is stained.

☐ Remove all magnets, photos, children's drawings, and the like from the front of the refrigerator. If there are a couple of truly necessary items, put them on the side of the refrigerator.

☐ Clean the stovetop and oven. Replace old burner pans if they are badly stained. Clean all exhaust fans, filters, and hoods.

☐ Clean the kitchen floor and keep it clean for showings.

☐ Keep the kitchen sink clean and empty on a daily basis.

☐ Make sure the kitchen faucet is working smoothly, without drips, and that it is clean.

☐ Clear everything off the window ledge above the kitchen sink.

☐ Remember to pack up the collections in the kitchen, too. Pack up your antique plate collection or whatever will distract buyers and take up space.

☐ Keep all soaps, towels, scouring pads, and cleaning supplies out of sight under the sink.

"You can't sell it if you can smell it."

—Barb Schwarz

☐ Some kitchens have too many scatter rugs in them. Too many rugs make a room look smaller. If space allows, one large Oriental rug in the middle of the kitchen looks great.

☐ Empty the garbage regularly to prevent kitchen odors.

☐ Move dog and cat dishes so that they don't interfere with buyers walking around the room.

MASTER BEDROOM

☐ Make the bed every day.

☐ Invest in a new bedspread if necessary.

☐ Clear off bedside tables and chests of drawers except for a very few necessary items like two or three magazines or books.

☐ Store extra books and magazines underneath the bed.

☐ Keep closet doors closed. If you have a walk-in closet, keep the floor clean and free of laundry and clutter.

☐ If you have a clock radio, keep it playing soft music during showings.

☐ Reduce the number of photos on tables and chests of drawers to a minimum.

HALLWAYS

☐ Remove plastic runners from carpet or hardwood floors.

ADDITIONAL BEDROOMS

Follow master bedroom guidelines.

☐ In children's rooms, take down all the posters except for one favorite over the bed. Repair nail holes and paint the walls.

LAUNDRY ROOM

☐ Put soaps and cleaners in a cupboard or reduce the number and organize them neatly on one shelf.

☐ Just as in the kitchen, keep counters and sinks clean and empty.

☐ Get rid of excess hangers and hanging laundry. If you have a drying area, replace all those miscellaneous hangers with one style of white plastic hangers.

☐ Make sure that lightbulbs are working and have adequate wattage. Many laundry rooms are too dark and need to be brighter.

BATHROOMS

☐ Clear off counters. Reduce toiletries to a decorative few (three to six) and consolidate them on a tray or in a basket. Put everything else in drawers or cabinets.

☐ Replace that ugly, dirty hand soap with a neat bottle of liquid soap.

☐ Coordinate all towels using one or two colors. Fold them in thirds and hang them neatly every day. New towels can be purchased very inexpensively if the ones you have don't match.

- [ ] Clear everything out of the shower and tub except for one bottle of liquid soap and one shampoo.
- [ ] Clean or replace the shower curtain. Keep shower curtains drawn at all times.
- [ ] One common problem in bathrooms is cracking or peeling just above the top of the shower tile or tub enclosure where it meets the drywall or ceiling. Repair, using caulking and paint, or install wood trim coated in polyurethane.
- [ ] Get rid of mold and stains throughout the bathroom, especially in the shower and bathtub area.
- [ ] Many tubs and showers need a fresh new bead of silicone caulking around the edges to make them look neat and clean.
- [ ] Remove all cloth toilet lid covers and water closet covers. Keep toilet lids down every day.
- [ ] Scatter rugs in front of the sink, toilet, and shower make the room look small. Use one larger rug in the middle of the room or none at all.
- [ ] Hide all cleaning supplies and the garbage can under the sink or out of the line of sight.

CLOSETS

- [ ] Make sure you can open the door freely without something falling out on a prospective buyer.

BASEMENTS

- [ ] Be aware of smells, musty odors, and dampness. Do your best to alleviate problems by repairing and cleaning problem areas. Use room deodorants and disinfectant sprays to help with any odors.

☐ If you use the basement for storage, condense the piles to one corner of one area of the basement.

☐ Repair any cracks in the ceilings and walls.

☐ Clear any drains.

OUTSIDE THE HOME

The first impression when a buyer drives up to your home is critical. Walk across the street and look at it through the eyes of a buyer. Be tough on yourself. What do you see?

TRIM AND HOUSE PAINT

☐ Take a hard look at the front door and trim. Give special attention to this because this is where buyers will get their first opportunity to make a close inspection of your home. Does it need repainting or staining? Repainting the doors and trim to help make the house look crisp and in good condition is one of the least expensive things you can do to dress up a home.

DECKS, PORCHES, AND PATIOS

☐ Sweep all decks, walks, porches, and patios and keep them swept.

☐ Remove any moss from all decks, walks, and patios.

☐ Decks should be pressure-washed, stained, or painted if they are in need of it.

☐ Reduce clutter on decks, porches, and patios so that they look bigger. Get rid of old flowerpots, barbecue equipment, charcoal, planters, toys, construction materials, and excess furniture.

☐ If you have outdoor furniture, create one simple room setting of *clean* furniture that will remind buyers of the usefulness of the space.

ROOF

☐ Clean all debris and moss from roof and gutters.

FENCES

☐ Repair broken fences and paint if necessary.

LANDSCAPING

☐ Plants are like children—they grow up so fast! First they are little and cute, then they seem just right, and all of a sudden they're so big we hardly know how to take care of them. You can't trim the kids, but you can trim your plants. If they need it, do it now.

"Buyers only know what they see, not how it's going to be."

—Barb Schwarz

☐ Rake and weed flowerbeds. If possible, spread new mulch such as beauty bark, pine needles, gravel, or lava rock to put a finishing touch on the landscaping.

☐ Remove dead plants.

☐ Mow the lawn and keep it mowed on a weekly basis during the growing season.

☐ Trim branches around the roofline to prevent animals, insects, and foliage from getting on the roof.

FRONT YARD

- ☐ Curb appeal is important. Has your landscaping overgrown the house? *Remember, you can't sell it if you can't see it!* Cut back to window height all shrubs that block light or view from windows. (If you're afraid they won't bloom next year, don't worry—you won't be there!)
- ☐ Move all children's toys to the backyard.
- ☐ Clean and sweep paved driveways. Rake, weed, or regravel driveways.

BACKYARD

- ☐ Remove any extra items from the yard, such as tools, piles of lumber, or auto parts.
- ☐ All children's toys should go in one area in the backyard.
- ☐ Clear any drainage grates.

GARAGE OR CARPORT

- ☐ Carports have to be completely cleaned out—everything!
- ☐ Garages should be swept out and organized. If you have to use part of or the entire garage for storage that's fine, just keep it neat.
- ☐ Always keep garage doors down while your home is on the market.
- ☐ If you're not using the garage for storage keep cars in the garage and not in the driveway.
- ☐ Move boats and RVs to a storage facility or a neighbor's home several homes away until your home sells.

Copyright © 2006 StagedHomes.com.

SHOWING YOUR STAGED HOME

EVERY DAY

Keep music playing throughout the house. Soft rock, popular, or light jazz are all appropriate.

Leave lights or lamps on to illuminate dark hallways and corners.

When an agent calls to show your home, ask the agent's name and the estimated time he or she will be showing. Ask the agent to please call you if he or she is running late or becomes unable to show your property as scheduled.

BEFORE ALL SHOWINGS

Set the stage: *Lights, music, action!*

- Open all curtains and blinds, unless otherwise advised.
- Turn on *all* lights and lamps.
- Close garage doors.
- Make sure all toilet lids are down.

201

- If it's hot outside, keep your house cool on the inside. If it's cold outside, keep the heat on inside your house even if it's vacant. Buyers won't stay in a house that's too hot or cold.
- Allow potential buyers privacy as they view your home. It is best to leave altogether, work in the yard, or take a nice long walk.

Remember, the way you live in a home and the way you market and sell your house are two different things.

Copyright © 2006 StagedHomes.com.

QUICK TIPS FOR STAGING YOUR HOME

Always look for an Accredited Staging Professional to list, Stage, market, and *sell* your home. Get ready to move. . . . *Start packing!*

Before you show your home to potential buyers, be sure to go through your whole house with your agent to finish the Staging process. Here are some quick tips to help you get started. Follow them, and your home will look better than the competition. Staged homes sell faster and/or for more money!

INSIDE

- Clear all unnecessary objects from furniture throughout the house. Keep decorative objects on the furniture restricted to groups of one, three, or five items. In general, a sparsely decorated home helps buyers mentally move in with their own things.
- Rearrange or remove some of the furniture in your home. Homeowners usually have too much furniture in a room. When you're selling your home, thin out overcrowded rooms to make them seem larger.

- Clear all unnecessary objects from the kitchen counter-tops. If something hasn't been used for three months, put it away! Clear refrigerator fronts of messages, magnets, pictures, and so on.
- In the bathroom, remove any unnecessary items from the countertops, tub, shower stall, and commode top. Keep only the most necessary cosmetics, brushes, perfumes, and the like, in one small group on the counter. Coordinate towels in one or two colors only.
- Take down, reduce, or rearrange pictures and objects on walls. Patch and paint all walls, if necessary.
- Review the house interior, room by room. Paint any room needing paint. Clean carpet and drapes that need it. And clean the windows.
- If you need room to store extra possessions, use the garage or rent a storage unit.
- During showings turn on *all* lights and lamps.
- Play pleasing music all day, every day.

OUTSIDE

- Go around the perimeter of the house and move all garbage cans, discarded wood scraps, extra building materials, and the like, to the garage, or, if appropriate, take them to the dump.
- Check gutters and roof for dry rot and moss.
- Make sure sidewalks and driveways are swept and cleaned.
- Prune bushes and trees. Keep plants from blocking windows: You can't sell a house if you can't see it!

- Remove dead plants, weed all planting areas, and put down fresh mulching material.
- Keep your lawn freshly cut, edged, and fertilized during the growing season.
- Clear patios or decks of all small items, such as little planters, flowerpots, charcoal, barbecue equipment, and toys.
- Check the condition of the paint on your home, especially the trim and the front door. The first impression, or curb appeal, is very important.

IN GENERAL

Try to look at your house through a buyer's eyes, as though you have never seen it before. This exercise will help you see what needs to be done. Any time and money invested on these items will usually bring you the return of more money and a quicker sale.

Working together, you and your Accredited Staging Professional make a *winning team*!

Copyright © 2006 StagedHomes.com.

INDEX